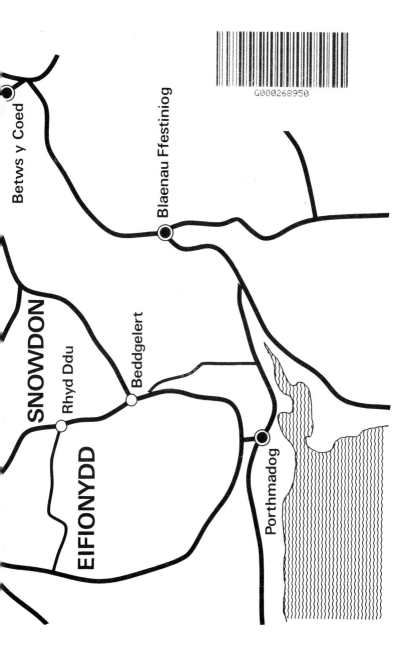

SCRAMBLES IN SNOWDONIA

SCRAMBLES IN SNOWDONIA

by

Steve Ashton

CICERONE PRESS
MILNTHORPE, CUMBRIA

Great Pinnacle Gap, Bristly Ridge (Route 27)

© Steve Ashton 1992
ISBN 1 85284 088 9
First published 1980
Reprinted 1981, 1984, 1988
Second Edition 1992, reprinted 1994, 1996

Acknowledgements

Many thanks to friends and strangers who have commented, good and bad, on the first edition of the guide. In particular I would like to thank Rob Collister, Jonathon Delamont, Jesse James and Malcom Webb for specific suggestions.

SA.

> **WARNING!**
> **SCRAMBLING CAN BE DANGEROUS**

PREFACE

What criteria should be used to define a scramble? General agreement could be reached on the lower limit - that we must also expect to use our hands on the rock - but fixing the upper limit is always going to be controversial. My own interpretation, reflected in the cut-off point for this guide, is that the technical interest of the climbing (which in any case ought not to exceed *Moderate* or *Just Difficult* standard in the rock climbing classification) must be superseded by the wider interests of scenery, position and atmosphere. In other words, seeking out difficulty for its own sake, without regard to line or position on the mountain, is not scrambling but rock climbing.

In preparation for this extensively re-written second edition I have re-climbed most of the routes, re-appraising grades and revising descriptions as necessary. I have also included another twenty-eight routes, extending the scope particularly on Tryfan and Glyder Fach. Significantly some of these are among the best routes in the guide, suggesting that many more worthwhile scrambles remain to be re-discovered.

Eleven years have elapsed since publication of the first edition of *Scrambles in Snowdonia*. In that time the book has served thousands of existing scrambling enthusiasts, and no doubt helped to convert many more from the ranks of hill walkers and rock climbers. This is not a comforting thought. Unroped scrambling, however exhilarating it may be, is potentially the most dangerous form of mountaineering. There have been times when - alone, unroped and in trouble half-way up some remote and uncharted face - I have vowed never to go into the mountains again. I break the vow regularly, but grow ever more cautious. There is no way of entirely eliminating the risk, only of reducing it. No mountain is worth a life, yet without mountains perhaps no worthwhile life remains to be lived.

Steve Ashton, 1992

Beneath Bear Tower on Bear Buttress (Route 69).
Crazy Pinnacle visible upper right

CONTENTS

Evening sunshine on the final arête of Braich Ty Du Face (Route 2)

INTRODUCTION

Area Covered by the Guide

All the described routes lie within the northern half of the Snowdonia National Park, where the most rugged mountains are found. Good scrambling in the southern half is scarce, the rock here being typically loose or vegetated.

Northern Snowdonia naturally divides into four regions. From north to south these are: the Carneddau, the Glyders, the Snowdon group and Eifionydd. The best scrambles will be found in the Glyders, with the large majority concentrated on Tryfan, Glyder Fach and Glyder Fawr. The Snowdon group also boasts many excellent routes, whereas the Carneddau and the Eifionydd regions provide only a handful.

Each region is introduced by a general description of the terrain and an indication of the scrambling potential, followed by some advice on valley bases, public transport and so on.

Maps

The entire area conveniently appears on the 1:50,000 OS Landranger Sheet 115 *Snowdon and Surrounding Area*. This map will suffice, though for greater detail consider buying *Snowdonia - Conwy Valley Area* and *Snowdonia - Snowdon Area* in the OS 1:25,000 Outdoor Leisure series.

Sketch maps accompanying this text merely assist in locating the regions and routes on the OS map, and are not substitutes for it.

Selection of Routes

The choice of routes is, by necessity and design, a selective one. All the best scrambles are included, though for the sake of a broader coverage some mediocre ones in the Glyders and Snowdon group have been omitted in favour of even poorer ones in the Carneddau and Eifionydd.

The range of difficulty extends from scrambly walks to the boundaries of proper rock climbing. Average fitness and a head for

11

heights will suffice at one end of the scale, whereas nothing short of mountaineer's skill and daring will do at the other. Some routes fit neither category: scrambling over loose rock and up dripping, vegetated gullies seems to require a special cunning, for which neither hill walking nor rock climbing provides adequate preparation. The proficient all-round scrambler is a unique beast, and probably lucky to be alive.

Route Descriptions

After a general introduction the description is divided into seven sections:

Summary: A concise description of the route for quick reference, useful when flicking through the guide looking for ideas.

Conditions: Use this information to find a route suitable for the prevailing weather conditions. An indication of popularity, rock quality and so on may also appear under this heading.

Approach: Suggests a suitable parking place with map reference and briefly describes the approach walk.

Ascent: Describes the route in ascent, generally or in detail according to the intricacy of the terrain. Remember that the described line is often only one of several ways of ascending the face. Use it as a guide, but be prepared to find easier or harder variations as the situation demands.

Descent by this route: Gives some special pointers when planning to use the route as a descent, or advises when a descent is impractical or unduly difficult.

Usual descents: Briefly describes walking or simple scrambling descents from the summit.

Combinations: Suggests interesting combinations of routes for those seeking a longer mountaineering day.

Route Classification

The routes have been classified 1,2 or 3, according to difficulty and level of risk. Borderline cases are indicated by a grade of 1/2 or

2/3. It is impossible to apply any grading system rigorously, and at best it can serve only as a rough guide.

Grade 1: This grade denotes routes which require no special mountaineering skills (eg. Snowdon Horseshoe, Tryfan North Ridge), and which should be within the capability of any adventurous and experienced hill walker. They are unlikely to require rope protection, and may be considered for descent or during doubtful weather.

Grade 2: Things are getting much more serious now. Routes include the difficult gullies and ridges, and the easier face routes (eg. Bryant's Gully, Clogwyn y Person Arête, Braich Ty Du Face). You may have to wait for optimum weather conditions, and even then difficulties which require rope protection may be encountered. A wide experience of scrambling, or a background in mountaineering, is essential. Such routes are rarely suitable for descent. Note also that a grade 2 climbed unroped may be potentially far more dangerous than a grade 3 climbed with rope protection.

Grade 3: These routes have the attributes of grade 2 scrambles but with the additional complication of one or more 'pitches' of simple rock climbing, on which rope protection is usual. Dry conditions are essential. Someone whose background is limited to hill walking and scrambling will need to acquire a knowledge of basic rope technique before attempting these routes, in particular an ability to select belay anchors, fix running belays, and, in the event of a forced retreat, to abseil.

Star Ratings

Routes have been allocated a quality rating from zero to three stars. Obviously this is a subjective assessment, though few will argue over the merits or otherwise of routes at either end of the scale:

    *** - Acknowledged classics, often crowded during weekends.

    ** - Routes of quality, sometimes unfrequented.

    * - Routes of merit but which lack continuous interest.

    No star - Poor routes described for completeness or because they are the best available in that particular region.

Route Illustrations

Route numbers in the text correspond to those indicated on the maps and photo-diagrams. It should be possible to locate and follow all scrambles using only an OS map and the route description. However, the photo-diagrams may help resolve an ambiguity. In some cases the starting point and line of a route is best indicated in plan form. In these cases an additional sketch map appears in the text.

Equipment

Clothing: Your normal hill walking clothing will generally be suitable for scrambling, but ensure that it gives adequate free movement for high leg and arm reaches. Knee-length waterproof jackets are a nuisance.

Fingerless wool gloves, useful for scrambling up cold or wet rock, will also afford some protection from rope burns while belaying and abseiling.

Footwear: Lightweight walking boots, particularly those with a firm rather than floppy midsole, are ideal for scrambling. Plastic mountaineering boots and other rigid-soled footwear are unnecessarily clumsy. Trainers and other ultra-light footwear may be adequate for the simple ridge scrambles but are useless in gullies and on the mixed ground of face routes.

Rucksack: Choose a neat daysack, ideally fitted with a stabilising waist strap but with as few other fittings as possible.

Rope: The rope most commonly used for mountaineering routes is of kernmantel construction, 45m long and 11mm in diameter. Such a rope can also be used for scrambling, though in most cases it will be unduly heavy and cumbersome to carry. At the other end of the scale, some people like to carry 15m of 9mm diameter rope for emergency purposes on the simple scrambles. Such a rope is light and convenient but far too short for the serious scrambles. The best compromise might be 36m of 9mm diameter climbing rope. This should be used double in ascent, allowing pitches of about 15m to be climbed between ledges with the option of making recoverable

15m abseils in an emergency. However, such a rope would be inadequate if used singly on longer pitches.

The rope must have a 'dynamic' quality (ie. it must be capable of stretching to help absorb the energy of a fall), so it is no use buying caving or yachting rope, which has a low-stretch 'static' quality. Go to a proper climbing shop and explain your needs. The rope should carry the UIAA label of approval. Note that rope sold off-the-reel in 8mm diameters or less for making into runners and slings is low-stretch 'static' rope and should not be used as a main rope for scrambling.

Other protection equipment: Three or four tape slings and karabiner clips will suffice for most routes. The slings may as well be of the full-strength 25mm width, preferably pre-stitched rather than knotted. Two of these should be of 2.4m length (these can then double as abseil sit-slings), the others may be of 1.2m. At least two of the karabiners ought to be of the locking type. All should conform to the current UIAA standard. If you intend using the Italian friction hitch method of belaying, then you will also need two HMS (pear-shaped) locking karabiners among the party.

All the scrambles described in this book can be minimally protected with this basic equipment. However, on some of the more technical routes you may wish to supplement the tape slings with three or four medium-sized nuts.

Helmets: The slight irritation experienced when wearing a climbing helmet must be weighed against the partial but valuable protection it offers against falling stones or glancing blows sustained during a fall. Wearing or not wearing a helmet is entirely a matter of personal choice. They are least useful when scrambling along ridges, and most useful in the confines of a scree-littered gully.

Basic Rope Technique

Instruction in rope technique is beyond the scope of this guide. Rock climbers and mountaineers will be able to adapt their normal belay methods to suit scrambling terrain. Hill walkers will need instruction from experienced companions. Failing that they may wish to enrol on a course at an outdoor centre (advertised in the specialist magazines) or to consult one of several textbooks. *The Hillwalker's Handbook* (Ashton, Crowood Press) includes a section devoted to rope-protected scrambles.

Access

Approaches have been carefully described to avoid crossing land where access is restricted or in dispute. Improvising unrecognised approaches across lower pastures merely antagonises farmers. Besides, there is plenty of scope for wandering at will on the higher ground.

Metric Units

Metric units for heights and distances have been used throughout, conforming to current OS metric maps. To convert to imperial measurements, think of metres as rather long yards, or, more accurately, multiply the height in metres by ten then divide by three for a close approximation in feet (eg. 60m=600/3=200ft). To convert from kilometres to miles, multiply by five then divide by eight (eg. 16km=80/8=10 miles).

A Final Cautionary Note

A guidebook of this sort reflects the author's own reactions and responses to the routes. Not everyone will agree on the exact lines to follow, the levels of difficulty encountered, or the best techniques to apply. I have climbed all the routes personally, specifically with the guide in mind, and at least once in every case without rope protection. Nevertheless, when faced by an unexpected route-finding problem you must be prepared to trust your own intuition.

The same goes for loose rock encountered on the routes. Coping with unstable blocks, shattered rock and treacherous vegetation is all part of the game. Even the easiest scrambles can never be made completely safe, and some are potentially more dangerous than most rock climbs.

All the described scrambles are 'summer' routes. Even the

simplest of them would be a totally different proposition in winter conditions, when ice-axe, crampons and winter-climbing skills are required. Remember that even when snow is absent the rocks may be coated in *verglas,* the thin veneer of ice rendering an ascent extremely difficult and dangerous.

Above all, scrambling demands good judgement of terrain and an ability to assess the potential risk at every stage. These skills are learned gradually, beginning with the grade 1 ridge scrambles. In this book I can suggest only where the routes go and give advice on how to overcome some of the obstacles you will meet. I can't decide for you whether or not it is safe to continue. Ultimately the choices and the adventures are yours.

CARNEDDAU

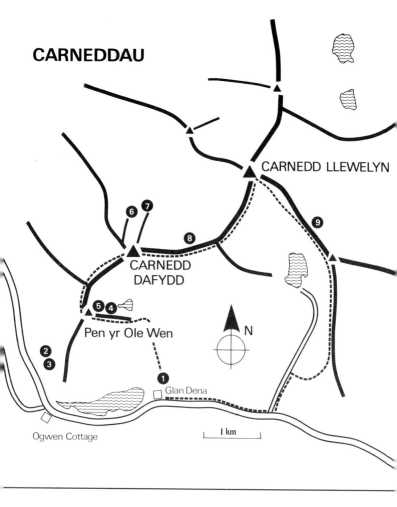

The Carneddau

The Carneddau form the most northerly hill group in Snowdonia. There are few hints here of the rocky intricacy of the Glyders, or the rugged splendour of Snowdon; impressions instead are of barren summits and remote valleys.

A fortunate arrangement of ridges means that, having once made the initial height gain, several summits can be strung together in a high-level horseshoe traverse. Unfortunately most of the scrambling potential lies dormant under a blanket of heather, and much of what escapes is either too difficult or too loose. Nevertheless, the few lines worth following are enriched by their remote settings.

In broad terms the group lies within a triangle defined by the coastline between Bangor and Conwy, and the valleys which extend inland from those towns towards Betws-y-Coed. More specifically, the area of particular interest lies to the north of the A5 between Llyn Ogwen and Capel Curig.

The main ridges are aligned roughly in the shape of a T, with Carnedd Llewelyn - the highest peak of the group - appropriately occupying the junction. These ridges and their major intervening cwms - Llugwy, Eigiau and Llafar - provide the usual means of access to the scrambles.

No single base serves all the routes, though with a bit of extra walking all can be reached from the Ogwen Valley between Capel Curig and Bethesda. Both villages offer basic amenities and a wide range of accommodation, including campsites (those with facilities are marked on OS maps, otherwise enquire locally), bunkhouses, youth hostels (Capel Curig and Idwal), bed and breakfast, and hotels. Regular rail and bus services link Conwy to Bangor and Betws-y-Coed. However, buses on the crucial Betws-y-Coed to Bethesda section operate infrequently outside peak holiday periods.

1: SOUTHERN RIDGE CIRCUIT *** (1)

This is the classic high-level ridge traverse of the Carneddau, and the best introductory outing in the group. Not only does it ascend four major peaks, but it also previews most of the routes described later in this section.

Scrambling interest is spaced, short-lived and of minimal difficulty, though anyone insisting on including something tougher in their mountain day could substitute one of Routes 2 to 5 for their ascent of Pen yr Ole Wen.

Summary: A ridge walk of five or six hours duration over four major Carneddau summits, punctuated by short, easy scrambles.

Conditions: Paths, mostly good, cross stony ground or grass. Much of the route is exposed to strong cross-winds, though nowhere is the ridge particularly narrow or precarious. Take care with route-finding on Carnedd Dafydd and Carnedd Llewelyn in mist. Wet rock does not significantly increase the difficulties. Although the route is very popular, the scrambling sections are too short to cause the hold-ups that sometimes afflict the equivalent horseshoe traverses on Snowdon and the Glyders.

Approach: Via the A5 from Capel Curig or Bethesda. Park on the roadside near the bridge at Glan Dena (GR:668 605).

Ascent/Descent: Follow the track past Glan Dena almost to Tal y Llyn Farm. Turn right on a path by a stone wall, later crossing the wall by a ladder stile. Follow the stream to the lake in Cwm Lloer with views ahead of the scrambles on Craig Lloer. Gain the left-bounding ridge of the cwm - the East Ridge - and ascend it, in its initial stages via a simple 7-8m scramble up a rock gully, to the summit of Pen yr Ole Wen.

Circle the rim of Cwm Lloer northwards and ascend a broad ridge to the summit of Carnedd Dafydd.

Descend east on a rocky path, then curve north around the rim of Cwm Llafar, finally rising to the summit of Carnedd Llewelyn with retrospective views of the Black Ladders and Llech Ddu.

Take the ridge south-east then east, passing around the head of the Craig yr Ysfa Amphitheatre, and descend by a 10m scramble over a gently angled rock nose to Bwlch Eryl Farchog (short-cut descent south from here to Ogwen). Scramble easily up the rocky ridge ahead to the summit of Pen yr Helgi Du.

Descend the grass ridge of Y Braich southwards. On passing through a gap in the transverse stone wall at GR:699 609, contour right then descend diagonally to cross the leat at a footbridge just left of a stone wall. Turn right and follow the leat to the surfaced Ffynnon Llugwy access road, which leads down to the A5 about 2km from the starting point.

PEN YR OLE WEN (978m)

The inelegant bulk of Pen yr Ole Wen protrudes south from the main mass of the Carneddau, introducing a kink into the Ogwen Valley where the outflow from Llyn Ogwen gushes down into the broad U-shaped valley of the Nant Ffrancon. For those based in the Ogwen Valley this is the most accessible of the Carneddau peaks, offering unrivalled views of the northern crags and cwms of the Glyders.

Unaccountably, the most popular walking route zig-zags up the unpleasant and exhausting south spur from Ogwen Cottage; connoisseurs choose the scenic and comparatively gentle East Ridge. An ascent of Pen yr Ole Wen by either route is generally regarded as a mere preliminary to a traverse of the higher Carneddau peaks.

The featureless south-east slope above Llyn Ogwen holds no interest for the scrambler, whereas the pseudo-alpine west (or Braich Ty Du) face, ribbed with ridges and riven with gullies, promises all sorts of adventure. Otherwise the best scrambling will be found at the head of Cwm Lloer, tucked out of sight behind the East Ridge.

2: BRAICH TY DU FACE * (2)
A huge, complex face of ribs and gullies rises above the Nant Ffrancon, appearing to provide endless opportunities for the scrambler. Unfortunately there are two main drawbacks: first, a large part of the lower slope consists of unstable scree which

21

*Exposed scrambling on the Pinnacle Ridge section of Braich Ty Du Face
(Route 2)*

threatens to cascade onto the road at the first ill-judged step and thus limits the choice of approach; and second, a wide band of heather at mid-height seriously affects continuity. The selected route does its best to avoid both scree and heather, though in doing so introduces route-finding difficulty of both large and small scale. If the intermittent ridge line seems contrived then it is for a good reason: ascending the face via the intervening grass couloirs would relieve none of the effort and monotony associated with the South Spur walking route.

Despite its shortcomings, the route redeems itself with some exciting situations and, on the upper face, a genuine sense of exploration.

Summary: Exposed scrambling on a pinnacled introductory ridge followed by tedious walking up open slopes of heather and grass. A discontinuous series of rock arêtes on the upper face leads with increasing difficulty to the summit slopes.

Conditions: West-facing and therefore a good choice when the north faces are likely to be cold or damp. Nevertheless, it is worth waiting for dry rock. Rock quality is generally good. Rock climbers or other scramblers are rarely encountered anywhere on this face.

Approach: Park at Ogwen Cottage (GR:649 604) or at overspill parking areas farther east. Leave the A5 at the Alfred Embleton stile, on the north side of the road bridge over the stream outlet from Llyn Ogwen. Turn left immediately after crossing the stile and follow the scrambly path onto a grass shoulder. The zig-zagging South Spur path up Pen yr Ole Wen now rises steeply above; follow it for just 20m or so then contour left, passing below buttresses on an intermittent path, to gain the slender Pinnacle Ridge which rises almost from the road and is topped by distinctive twin pinnacles. Fifteen minutes.

A more direct approach to the upper face can be made by walking half-way up the South Spur path, to where it zig-zags to avoid a prominent 30m-high crag, then contouring left onto the central heather band. However, some difficulty may then be experienced in locating the Porcupine Ridge - the key to the upper face.

Ascent: A grass ramp and short staircase lead naturally onto Pinnacle Ridge from about 10m above the stone wall which crosses the right-bounding couloir a little above its base. Follow the crest to a ledge then ascend a 3m step, slightly on the right using large holds, to gain another ledge. An exposed traverse of the pinnacles, often taken on their couloir flanks, then leads to a heather shoulder and slender grass col.

The next objective is the cluster of ribs seen on the left side of the upper face. A broad couloir above and slightly left of the Pinnacle Ridge exit avoids a blocky buttress and emerges onto an open slope of grass and heather. Plod up this to a line of low, broken outcrops then take a rising leftward line to gain the left skyline ridge (which, without stretching our imagination too far, we could call the Porcupine).

Some of the Porcupine spines can be dodged, but soon the rocks coalesce into a continuous rib and, after a few difficult metres, the outlook suddenly becomes more serious. It is now best to cross the gully on the left and gain the ridge beyond.

Start the second ridge via a grass groove on the left, returning to the crest after about 25m. Some of this is quite awkward. Although the line now attempts to stay near the crest, blank slabs force frequent diversions, usually to the left. Detailed route-finding here is quite involved.

Eventually the ridge falls back into a knife edge and finally turns to grass as it abuts against the supporting mass of the mountain. The path of the South Spur walking route is close by and soon leads to the summit.

Descent by this route: Not recommended.

Usual descents: The knee-wrecking South Spur provides the quickest and most convenient return to the start. Otherwise descend by the East Ridge (refer to Route 1).

Combinations: It is a pity to waste hard-won altitude so this route makes an excellent alternative start to a traverse of the Carneddau ridges (Route 1).

Braich Ty Du Face of Pen yr Ole Wen

3: BRAICH TY DU FACE RIGHT-HAND START * (2/3)

Merely an alternative start to the preceding route, and fares no better in avoiding the heather bashing in the middle of the face.

Summary: Difficult scrambling on an introductory buttress followed by tedious walking up open slopes of heather and grass. A discontinuous series of rock arêtes on the upper face leads with increasing difficulty to the summit slopes.

Conditions: In general as for Route 2, though the introductory buttress is more vegetated and therefore tends to hold drainage. Wait for dry conditions.

Approach: As for Route 2. Shortly before reaching the distinctive Pinnacle Ridge, a dry stone wall cuts across the traversing approach path. Follow the wall up to the base of a broad-fronted buttress. (Refer also to Route 2 for a more direct approach to the upper face.) Fifteen minutes.

Ascent: Ascend steep grass on the left side of the buttress for about 25m, passing a tree half-way, to within about 5m of a larger tree. Scramble rightwards over rock ledges set beneath an overhanging wall towards the buttress crest. A high-angled and heather-filled break offers only a slim chance of upward progress so instead traverse heather ledges to the right (deceptively difficult and so worth roping-up for) to enter a simple chimney/gully which leads up to a notch on the true crest.

Step up from the notch and ascend slabby rock for 5m or so then move to the right, crossing a rock rib. Ascend heather ledges above, moving left after a few metres to gain a pinnacle on the rib crest. Scramble up the remains of the rib to emerge on slopes of heather and gorse. Ascend these laboriously, trending left to join Route 2 at the line of low, broken outcrops.

Continue as for Route 2 to the summit.

Descent by this route: Not recommended.

Usual descents: As for Route 2.

Combinations: As for Route 2.

Pinnacle Ridge section of Braich Ty Du Face

4: BROAD GULLY RIDGE (1/2)

Easy-angled rock on the inner flank of Pen yr Ole Wen is generally too vegetated for worthwhile scrambling. This route is no exception, so its main purpose is to prolong time spent within the enchanting hollow of Cwm Lloer. Its merits should be judged accordingly.

Near the left side of the craggy headwall the prominent couloir of Broad Gully extends from the floor of the cwm to the crest of the East Ridge. This route begins up the couloir then ascends the blunt and heathery ridge to its left.

Summary: Unattractive scrambling in an attractive setting up a heathery ridge.

Conditions: This is an unpopular and vegetated north-facing crag and so the rocks, though generally reliable, are lichenous and often greasy.

Approach: Via the A5 from Capel Curig or Bethesda. Park on the roadside near the bridge at Glan Dena (GR:668 605). Follow the track past Glan Dena almost to Tal y Llyn Farm. Turn right on a path by a stone wall, later crossing the wall by a ladder stile. Follow the stream to the lake in Cwm Lloer. Forty minutes.

Ascent: Avoid the first awkward step of the ridge by ascending Broad Gully almost to the constriction at the start of the gully proper. Here a 15m-long grassy rut cuts up left to the ridge. The rut turns nasty at half height so exit via rock steps on the left to a shoulder of grass and heather (which could have been gained more easily via boulder and heather slopes on the left, but never mind).

Above some easy scrambling a prominent tower of compact rock bars the way. Ascend awkwardly over piled boulders just to its left (or make other arrangements even farther left) then romp over boulders and heather, becoming more difficult, to a scree shoulder.

Continue via a shallow couloir to exit onto the East Ridge, or divert left (hard) or right (easier) for a final flourish on rock. The upper part of the East Ridge leads to the summit in about ten minutes.

Descent by this route: Not recommended.

Usual descents: By the East Ridge to the entrance of Cwm Lloer.

Alternatively, descend steeply-angled grass and scree at the head of the cwm, flanking the north side of Craig Lloer in the lower part.

Combinations: Useful as an alternative start to a traverse of the Carneddau ridges (Route 1).

5: CRAIG LLOER SPUR * (2/3)

Sustained scrambling begins and ends on the compact buttress of Craig Lloer, a triangular crag truncating the shallow spur which protrudes into the head of the cwm. Though short-lived, the difficult section is enjoyable and, in places, exhilaratingly exposed. Unfortunately the upper part of the spur involves little more than steep walking.

The traverse proves to be the key to an ascent of the buttress and, given that a false line will lead to difficulties, must be identified beyond doubt. However, an escape is available before the traverse for those unfamiliar with what are essentially rock climbing situations.

Summary: Ascends a spur which rises from a delightfully secluded cwm, initially by some difficult and exposed scrambling on its truncating cliff.

Conditions: Craig Lloer faces north-east and so catches the morning sun. It takes little drainage and so dries much more quickly than the neighbouring Broad Gully Ridge. Rock quality is good and vegetation does not interfere, though it is worth waiting for dry conditions. The route is not widely popular.

Approach: As for Route 4 to the entrance of Cwm Lloer. From the west shore of the lake, ascend to below the centre of Craig Lloer then struggle up scree, passing a grass bay, to the edge of the crag near the entrance to its left-bounding gully (in fact a broad couloir with several branches). Forty-five minutes.

Ascent: Avoid a group of tilted blocks at the foot of the ridge via a 6m slab on the right (the block can be avoided more easily on the left, though the slab gives a useful foretaste of the difficulties to come).

Above, ignore easy ground to the left and ascend over small blocks to a larger one split by a 3m crack. Good holds reward a

confident step up the crack, and there are large belay spikes above if required. Continue easily for 12m or so until stopped by a slabby but hopelessly smooth wall (the last escape into the couloir).

From a belay block, traverse heather ledges rightwards to their end (if roping this section, you will now find a large spike a couple of metres higher for sling protection). Continue the traverse via a hand-rail flake to arrive at a notch on the right edge in a position of breathtaking exposure. When ready, pull up then mantelshelf (or belly flop) onto a flat ledge with a block belay beyond. The major difficulties are now over.

The apex of the buttress is not far above; gain it via heathery scrambling and a few interesting moments on curious, knobbly rock. The tedious scree of the broader upper spur leads to a simple scrambling exit through the final barrier wall to gain the East Ridge path near the summit.

Descent by this route: Not recommended.

Usual descents: By the East Ridge to the entrance of Cwm Lloer. Alternatively, descend steeply-angled grass and scree at the head of the cwm, flanking the north side of Craig Lloer in the lower part.

Combinations: Useful as an alternative start to a traverse of the Carneddau ridges (Route 1).

CARNEDD DAFYDD (1044m)

Despite its great bulk, Carnedd Dafydd asserts its character only on the north-western approach through Cwm Llafar. Viewed from elsewhere its summit and flanks blend into the high ground of a ridge system which links the six highest Carneddau peaks. Rarely is it ascended for its own sake.

Scrambling interest is confined to the north face of the mountain - the Cwm Llafar flank. This headwall, evocatively named Black Ladders, is one of the most dramatic in Snowdonia. Though a rich source of winter climbs, its dripping tiers of rock do not invite

Craig Lloer Spur, Pen yr Ole Wen

attention in summer. Only on neighbouring Llech Ddu, the truncating cliff of Crib Lem, will you see rock climbers, and then only during the driest weather. With one exception the scrambling is disappointing, most of the obvious lines being either too vegetated or too loose for full enjoyment. Remoteness and atmosphere compensate.

6: CWMGLAS BACH SPUR (1 or 2)

Poor scrambling in a tremendous setting. Of use mainly to those determined to find an alternative to Crib Lem, to which it bears a superficial resemblance. There is not much scrambling by the easiest route, while even the harder direct variants are escapable.

Summary: Steep walking or scrappy scrambling to gain a broad, reclining ridge of rock and grass.

Conditions: North-facing at high altitude and so often wet. The easiest line is not badly affected by wet conditions, unlike the direct with its lichenous and mossy rock. Not popular.

Approach: As for Route 7 to the hollow of Cwmglas Bach, above and to the right of Llech Ddu - the truncating crag of Crib Lem. One hour.

Ascent: The spur terminates in Craig y Cwmglas Bach, which offers no hope of a direct scrambling approach, either up The Gully - the central green cleft - or its main right-hand buttress. However, some sort of flanking route is possible on the left-hand Pillar Buttress.

From the base of The Gully, take a rising leftward line on grass and rock, just below the steep upper wall, for 50m or so. Now work back right above the wall (Grade 2 unless a couple of awkward steps are avoided on the left) to gain the knife-edged crest of the buttress. All this can be avoided by taking an ungraded line much farther left.

From a slight col, where the buttress crest joins the main bulk of the mountain, follow a sheep track rightwards - across the top of The Gully - to a grass shoulder above the main buttress of the crag. The broad, upper ridge now rises above. Avoid the first step on the right, or take it direct with a struggle (2). Continue up the crest with minimal amounts of scrambling onto the stones of the summit dome.

High above remote Cwm Llafar on Crib Lem (Route 7), Carnedd Dafydd

Descent by this route: A feasible descent by the easier variants, though difficult to locate in mist from the convex summit slopes. Most steps of the upper ridge can be avoided on the left (looking out), and all the lower difficulties can be avoided by descending diagonally rightwards (looking out) from the crest of Pillar Buttress.

Usual descents: As for Route 7.

Combinations: As for Route 7.

7: CRIB LEM (LLECH DDU SPUR) *** (1)

An enchanting approach to Carnedd Dafydd through the long, secluded valley of Cwm Llafar abruptly changes to one of menace at the point where Llech Ddu towers above the path. This compact 100m-high cliff guards entry to a long, low-angled ridge of alternating rock and grass arêtes that leads directly to the summit. Flank the cliff and this line - the finest scramble in the Carneddau - is yours.

Summary: Simple, perfectly situated scrambling on the short and comparatively safe steps of a prominent ridge leading directly to the summit of Carnedd Dafydd.

Conditions: Despite its north-facing aspect and high altitude, the ridge sheds drainage quickly. The rock is generally reliable, and the route's new-found popularity keeps it clear of moss and lichen.

Approach: Turn uphill off the A5 at crossroads at the eastern extremity of Bethesda. Turn right at crossroads in 1km and find a parking place on the narrow lane, taking care not to obstruct gates or passing places. Continue along this lane to the waterworks gate and cross a stile on the right. Cross a second stile at the top left corner of the field, and a third shortly after. Follow the track to open ground. Take the path, vague at first, which ascends parallel to the Afon Llafar to enter Cwm Llafar. Continue by a good path to huge boulders below the crag of Llech Ddu (GR:666 637). Ascend to the right of the crag to enter the hollow of Cwmglas Bach. One hour.

Ascent: Resist gaining the crest of the spur directly and instead ascend into the cwm almost to the level of the gully which splits Craig y Cwmglas Bach, at which point a ramp of grass and stones

On the approach to Tryfan's North Ridge via the Milestone Continuation, (Route 23)

slanting diagonally left between bands of rock will be revealed. It leads without complication to a bilberry shoulder on the spur above Llech Ddu.

Ascend through seemingly compact rock on the right side of the broad frontage to gain the narrower and less steeply inclined upper crest. Follow the crest over several knife edges and short steps to the stony summit dome.

Descent by this route: A reasonable proposition once located. When peering down from the convex summit slopes, several similar-looking spurs can be seen protruding into the cwm. Crib Lem protrudes furthest. A band of scree across the broad lower spur signals the approach of Llech Ddu and the need to bear left (looking out) to find the grassy ramp leading into Cwmglas Bach.

Usual descents: (i) To return to Gerlan, descend north-west from the summit along the delightful Cwm Llafar Ridge, joining the approach path at the entrance to the cwm. (ii) To return to the foot of the cliffs, descend the ridge eastwards until well beyond the Black Ladders headwall and then descend grass and boulder slopes into the head of Cwm Llafar.

Combinations: Follow the main Carneddau ridge path around the head of Cwm Llafar to the summit of Carnedd Llewelyn and complete the 'Cwm Llafar Horseshoe' by returning to the mouth of the cwm via Yr Elen.

8: EASTERN RIDGE OF BLACK LADDERS (2)

The upper basin of Cwm Llafar terminates in the crescent walls of the Black Ladders. Upper ridge crests glow attractively in the afternoon sun while shady lower walls ooze ugliness and impregnability. Almost no-one comes here in summer. The solitary scramble on this face has been forced to take the loose and moss-covered rock of the left-bounding buttress which, broad and poorly-defined, only gathers itself into a recognisable line at two-thirds height. The atmosphere, though sadly not the scrambling, is terrific.

Summary: A long, pleasant approach to the headwall of a remote cwm ascended by the loose and frequently damp rocks of a high-angled buttress.

Conditions: North-facing at high altitude and so often wet. The rock is not only unreliable but lichenous, so it's worth waiting for dry conditions. Rarely climbed.

Approach: As for Route 7 to the huge boulders below Llech Ddu. Continue towards the head of the cwm over man-trapping boulders then trend left to arrive beneath the easternmost rocks of the face. One hour fifteen minutes.

Ascent: A broad-based buttress tapering to a ridge defines the left side of the Black Ladders. As elsewhere on the cliffs, horizontal bands of rock prevent a direct approach to the foot of the buttress proper. They are best flanked on the left followed by a rising traverse back right. This approach gains the buttress at the same level as the start of East Gully, the foot of which is also terminated prematurely by banding.

Though there are many possible lines to take on the buttress, even the easiest of them involves some awkward mossy steps. A little higher the ridge divides: the right fork curves farther right, overlooking the gully, while the left continues directly, narrowing, and is perhaps the best choice. A final steepening can be avoided on the left via some loose blocks.

The route emerges suddenly onto level ground with the main Carneddau ridge path near by. The summit of Carnedd Dafydd lies a few minutes away to the west.

Descent by this route: Not recommended.

Usual descents: As for Route 7.

Combinations: As for Route 7.

CARNEDD LLEWELYN (1064m)

Carnedd Llewelyn, highest peak of the group, occupies a key position at the junction of the two major Carneddau pathways. Its four supporting ridges are aligned approximately south, west, north and east. The southern ridge drops gently to the shallow col of Bwlch Cyfryw Drum (descent into Cwm Llafar possible from here) before curving east above the cliffs of Black Ladders and rising to the summit of Carnedd Dafydd. The short west ridge drops only to a high col before rising again to the summit of Yr Elen, a major satellite peak. The north ridge extends in gradual descent towards Foel Grach, Foel Fras and the gentle hills beyond. Finally, the east ridge curves south-east, passing above the cliffs of Craig yr Ysfa, and dips to the pronounced col of Bwlch Eryl Farchog before rising again to the summit of Pen yr Helgi Du. All ridges apart from the west ridge carry well-used paths.

The only face of any real interest to the scrambler is that of Craig yr Ysfa, which lies some distance from the summit on the flanks of the east/south-east ridge. The cliff is hidden from most viewpoints, and so a special effort is required even to inspect what is on offer. There is even an unlikely story which would have us believe the cliff was discovered by telescope from Scafell.

Though the cliffs are extensive, heather covers much of the easier-angled rock, while loose rock or vegetation fills the most promising gullies. The selected scramble avoids the worst by finding a comparatively uncomplicated exit from the huge central Amphitheatre. The Amphitheatre is in fact a deep, square-cut recess set above a sloping bed of scree. It is bounded on the right by a 90m-high vertical wall of superb rock - host to some of the best Carneddau rock climbs - and on the left by the 300m-long terraced rib of Amphitheatre Buttress - a classic low-standard rock climb.

9: CRAIG YR YSFA AMPHITHEATRE * (2)

Hopes for an easy exit from Craig yr Ysfa's Amphitheatre fade when the options are viewed from the gloomy confines of its scree bed. None of the lines on the headwall appears free of complication. The right-hand gully presents the least number of obstacles so received the honour of selection, though some may feel the route lacks stature for so majestic a setting. Only the lower part of the route involves any technical scrambling, although care is required throughout.

Summary: A long approach into the central ravine of a remote cliff escaped via slabs, a short gully and a natural staircase of rock steps.

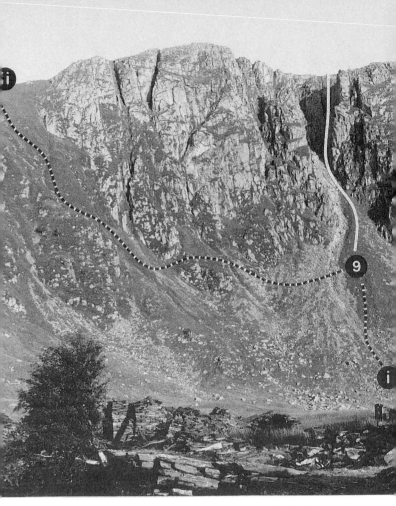

Craig yr Ysfa Amphitheatre and approaches, Carnedd Llewelyn

Conditions: The cliff faces east so gets the morning sun in summer. Takes comparatively little drainage. The rock is mainly sound on the difficult bits, but take care not to dislodge or receive debris from the easier sections - especially during summer weekends when the crag may be busy (the route is sometimes descended by climbing parties approaching the Lower Amphitheatre Wall).

Approach: (i) Via Cwm Eigiau. From Tal y Bont on the B5106 between Conwy and Llanrwst, follow a road rising westwards out of the village (not the road to Llanbedr-y-cennin) for about 5km. Park at the roadhead at the entrance to Cwm Eigiau (GR:732 663), taking care not to obstruct the gate. Walk along a rough track to the Llyn Eigiau dam and cross the outflow. Continue by the lakeside track and follow it through the cwm to its terminus at ruined quarry buildings. Cross marshland and ascend the scree fan to enter the central ravine of the Amphitheatre (GR:694 637). One hour thirty minutes. (ii) From the A5 in the Ogwen Valley. Park in a lay-by at the start of the reservoir access road at GR:688 603. Walk up towards Ffynnon Llugwy but leave the road where it veers left towards the lake outflow. Continue by the path which rises to the prominent col of Bwlch Eryl Farchog. Descend heather slopes leftwards (looking out) on the far side then follow a path down runnels and heather ribs, still trending left, to gain the scree fan below the Amphitheatre. One hour forty-five minutes.

Ascent: The broad, scree-covered Amphitheatre bed rises steeply to the broken headwall, at the right-hand side of which will be found a short gully pitch with slabs to its left. Use the slabs to gain a small recess above the nasty gully pitch.

The recess has two exits. The one on the left leads to a loose gully, so exit right via the good holds of a short wall. Step left above the wall to a clean, slanting slab in more open ground.

From the slab, rock steps lead naturally onto a series of clean rock staircases which zig-zag up the otherwise loose and unpleasant terrain of the easing headwall.

Turn right to follow the ridge path up to the summit of Carnedd Llewelyn.

Descent by this route: Not recommended without prior knowledge of the route. Take care to find and follow the staircases on the upper section, which even then can be intimidating.

Usual descents: (i) From the top of Craig yr Ysfa. After emerging from the Amphitheatre, turn left and follow the ridge path, via a simple scramble down a rock nose, to Bwlch Eryl Farchog. Refer to the approach notes for continuing the descent into Cwm Eigiau or the Ogwen Valley. (ii) Alternative descent from Carnedd Llewelyn to the Ogwen Valley. From the summit, descend the ridge south-west over Bwlch Cyfryw Drum then take the subsidiary ridge south-east (avoiding terminating crags on their south side) to the Ffynnon Llugwy outflow and access road. (iii) Descent from Carnedd Llewelyn to Cwm Eigiau. Descend the ridge northwards towards Foel Grach then turn right to descend a blunt subsidiary grass spur. From the grass plateau, descend due south into Cwm Eigiau, arriving in the vicinity of the ruined quarry buildings.

Combinations: For a more interesting return to the Ogwen Valley, follow Route 1 in reverse over Carnedd Dafydd and Pen yr Ole Wen.

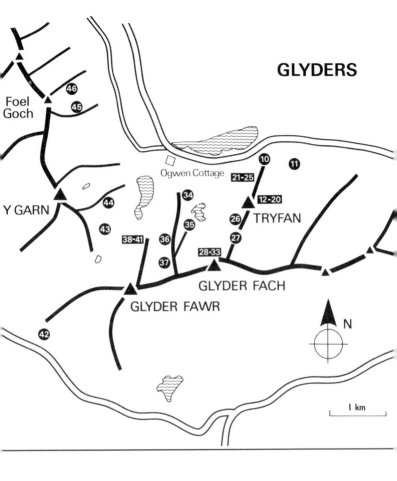

The Glyders

Predictably the finest scrambling in North Wales is to be found in the Glyders, either within rock-walled cwms or along the crests of intervening ridges. Hence the large number of routes described in this section.

The medium is almost always reliable, rotten rock and treacherous vegetation being limited to a small number of notorious cliffs. However, a continuing popularity means that favourite routes, stripped of grass and lichen, have become skeletal in character.

The mountains described in this section - the two Glyders and neighbouring Tryfan, Y Garn and Foel Goch - occupy the high ground between the Llanberis and Ogwen valleys. In simplified terms the range consists of a string of summits lying parallel to the A5 between Bethesda and Capel Curig, the exception being the satellite peak of Tryfan.

A complex arrangement of ridges and hanging valleys shape the northern flank of the main backbone of the range, which elsewhere is characterised by featureless slopes of heather and boulders. Not surprisingly, interest focuses on the north side.

A base in the Ogwen Valley is best. For those with private transport, anywhere between Capel Curig and Bethesda will do. Both villages provide basic amenities and a wide range of accommodation, including campsites (those offering facilities are marked on OS maps; enquire locally for other sites), bunkhouses, youth hostels (Capel Curig and Idwal), bed and breakfast, and hotels. Bus services along roads encircling the Glyders are extremely limited except in summer, when the Sherpa buses operate.

10: CWM BOCHLWYD HORSESHOE *** (1)

This exhilarating ridge traverse, similar in quality and difficulty to the Snowdon Horseshoe, provides an ideal introduction to scrambling. In circling Cwm Bochlwyd it visits the summits of Tryfan and Glyder Fach; ascends two classic ridges - the North Ridge of Tryfan and Bristly Ridge on Glyder Fach; and descends two lesser ones - the South Ridge of Tryfan and the Gribin Ridge. All these components of the traverse are described separately later, but for convenience are summarised below.

Summary: A horseshoe ridge traverse of about six hours duration incorporating two of the finest scrambles in the Glyders.

Conditions: Extremely popular during fine summer weekends, so start early or late to avoid crowds. The highly polished rock -

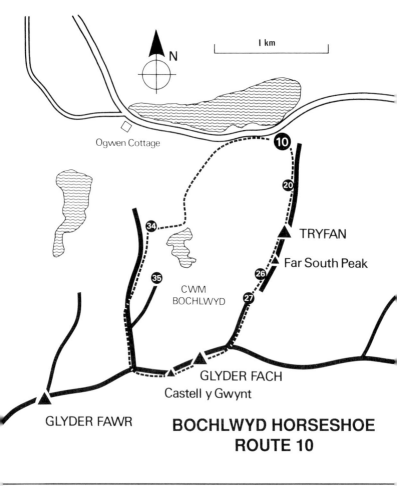

BOCHLWYD HORSESHOE ROUTE 10

unpleasant though not especially difficult to climb when wet - soon dries after rain during warm or breezy weather. Bristly Ridge is exposed to strong cross-winds.

Approach: From Capel Curig or Bethesda along the A5. Park in the lay-by (GR:663 603) below the Milestone Buttress, a prominent feature on the lower west side of the North Ridge.

Ascent/Descent:

(i) *Ascent of Tryfan via the North Ridge (Route 20):* From the lay-by, ascend near a stone wall then trend left before reaching the Milestone Buttress to gain a shoulder on the North Ridge. Ascend a boulder slope and break through a short barrier at its top. Continue slightly on the left side of the broad ridge to a quartz platform (the Cannon will be found over on the right). Scramble up the next high barrier near its left side and continue to another large platform below a prominent nose. Scramble up the nose on polished rock to its summit and descend to a notch on the far side (or avoid the nose by traversing its left side to the north). Escape the notch by trending right and then ascend a gully to the North Summit. Continue easily over boulders to the twin standing stones of Adam and Eve on the Central Summit.

(ii) *Descent of Tryfan via the South Ridge (Route 26):* Traverse to the South Summit then descend the South Ridge, generally by its gentler west side, to the broad col between South and Far South Summits. Again avoid difficulties by flanking the South Summit on the west side and then descend to Bwlch Tryfan (GR:662 588).

(iii) *Ascent of Glyder Fach via Bristly Ridge:* Follow the stone wall to the base of the first crags of Bristly Ridge. Ascend a short gully 10m to the right, exiting left over a man-made wall to the foot of a more imposing gully. Ascend the gully, detouring left where it steepens, to easier ground. Continue up a slabby shoulder to a narrowing of the ridge. Scramble over a small pinnacle onto a larger one then descend into a prominent notch on the ridge - Great Pinnacle Gap. Escape by a short wall just right of the slender Great Pinnacle then pass through a gap between a squat pinnacle and the main body of the ridge to reach easier ground leading up to the summit plateau. Walk south-west to join the normal ascent path and follow it to the summit of Glyder Fach.

(iv) *Descent from Glyder Fach via the Gribin Ridge (Route 34)* From the summit, continue south-west - scrambling around or over Castell y Gwynt - to Bwlch y Ddwy Glyder (GR:652 582). Ignore the continuation of the path to Glyder Fawr and instead circle the rim of Cwm Bochlwyd onto the promontory above the Gribin Ridge. Descend the ridge, initially by some simple scrambling near the crest (avoid straying too far down the west flank), to a level section. Continue along the east side of the ridge until a path curves right and descends to the Llyn Bochlwyd outflow. Descend the path on the west bank of the stream then cross it for a rightward diagonal descent over boggy ground to gain the A5 at a large car park (GR:659 601) less than 500m from the start.

TRYFAN (915m)

Tryfan's distinctive shape dominates the view when approaching Llyn Ogwen from either direction along the A5 road. Pundits say you can't climb the mountain without at some point using your hands for support. Two erect monoliths, Adam and Eve, tip the spectacular summit; daring extroverts will entertain the gathering by attempting the traditional leap from one to the other.

The backbone of Tryfan is composed of two ridges. The more prominent North Ridge descends towards the A5 road and east shore of Llyn Ogwen, while the shorter and less dramatic South Ridge provides a link to Glyder Fach. The faces which support this spine - east and west - are both impressively rocky. The ascent route most used by walkers approaches from Ogwen Cottage via Cwm Bochlwyd then takes the South Ridge by its west side.

Above the prominent ramp of the Heather Terrace which slants across the East Face stands a series of high buttresses separated by deep gullies. These are the lines of the best known rock climbs and scrambles on the mountain. Apart from the accessible Milestone Buttress, the huge but heather-choked West Face has been largely ignored by both rock climbers and scramblers.

11: TRYFAN BACH APPROACH *** (3)
Thousands of would-be climbers first clutch at ropes and rock on the slabby wedge of Tryfan Bach. Hardly the stuff of mountain scrambling, yet there are good reasons for including an ascent as a prelude to a day on the East Face of Tryfan. First, the line of deep

Tryfan Bach, prelude to Tryfan's East Face,

cracks up the left side of the slabs - the easiest genuine rock climb in North Wales - is the ideal route on which to practise rope techniques that might be required on more serious grade 3 scrambles. Second, it enlivens an otherwise tedious approach to the Heather Terrace.

The ascent is split into two stages: a climb of 60m or so up the left side of the forty-five-degree main slab, followed by a ridge scramble to the crag summit. Most parties will want to climb the whole of the first section in roped pitches. The best belay ledges are about 25m apart, though intermediate stances can be found if necessary (these are indicated in the description). It is worth carrying three or four medium-sized chocks in addition to the usual selection of slings.

Summary: An exciting alternative approach to Tryfan's East Face. Exposed and sustained rock scrambling on the large, polished holds of a slabby face followed by more varied scrambling up a blunt ridge.

Conditions: The slab faces west and so catches the sun from midday onwards. The clean rock soon dries out after rain, though the difficult step on the upper ridge could remain greasy for some time. The slab section seethes with novice rock climbers on summer afternoons.

Approach: From the A5 between Capel Curig and Bethesda. Roadside parking on the long straight east of Llyn Ogwen. From the farm of Gwern Gof Uchaf (GR:673 604), follow the signed path (stile) south-west to the obvious slab-fronted crag. Ten minutes.

Ascent: The route is based on a series of deep cracks near the left side of the face. Start 10m right of the left edge of the slabs and follow an obvious break slanting diagonally left to a large ledge with sling and nut belay. (10m)

Ignore the difficult direct line above and resume the leftward diagonal to gain a smaller ledge with sling and nut belay. (5m)

The rock steepens above and there's a tricky step-up 3m right of the slab edge to regain the crack line. A sentry box stance with good belays arrives soon. (10m)

Continue in the same line, trending right where the slab curves across so as to maintain a 3m separation from its edge, to reach a broken area near the crest. (15m)

Scramble up a 5m chimney to gain the broad ridge crest and ascend it without great difficulty by polished grooves to a spacious grass shoulder. (There's an easy descent to the foot of the slabs via the grass furrow on the west side here, and an easy way to the top of the crag by a flanking route on the left.)

Scramble up to below the final nose of the ridge (take care with the belay here) and enter a steepening groove. Both direct and leftward exits are difficult so, just below the steepening (nut runner), use a crack and large foothold on the right wall to balance across to a blunt spike. Block belay above.

Easy scrambling soon leads to the top of Tryfan Bach with a good view of the approach to Tryfan's East Face.

Descent by this route: Not recommended.

Usual descents: Descend by a path on the grassy east side to return direct to the road, or by a rocky path below the slabs of the west side to return to the start.

Combinations: Use as an approach to any of the scrambles on Tryfan's East Face (Routes 12 to 20).

12: BASTOW BUTTRESS VARIANT ** (2/3)

This is the first worthwhile route encountered on the Heather Terrace approach, and therefore a good choice for the impatient. The route finishes far short of the summit, but at least arrives on the North Ridge below the best scrambling.

The buttress consists of a typical East Face mix of rock ribs and heather runnels, though some of the situations are uniquely exciting.

Summary: Frequently difficult scrambling on a series of discontinuous rock ribs interspersed with heather. Easy scrambling up the popular North Ridge to finish.

Conditions: The rock, lichenous through lack of traffic, is not as reliable as most on Tryfan. Dry conditions are essential. The buttress takes little drainage and faces the morning sun .

Approach: From the A5 between Capel Curig and Bethesda. Roadside parking on the long straight east of Llyn Ogwen. From the farm of Gwern Gof Uchaf (GR:673 604), follow the signed path (stile) south-

East Face of Tryfan

49

west to the obvious slab-fronted crag of Tryfan Bach. Ascend to the right of the crag to a fence erected across the mouth of Cwm Tryfan. Now go right to ascend a badly eroded scree gully, emerging at a level area on the right. Cross the top of the gully onto the indistinct beginnings of the Heather Terrace. Beyond a rise the main buttresses come into view, and soon after the terrace assumes its true character. Cross the first water course (No Gully - a shallow runnel of heather, grass and stones) and continue below crags to the first proper gully: a deep one between rock walls, floored with large stones. This is Bastow Gully (1/2), a poor route consisting mainly of scree plodding with one rise at two-thirds height. One hour.

Ascent: From about 10m up Bastow Gully (above its first small step), follow an obvious break slanting rightwards - with a brief struggle to get past the first chockstone - towards the ridge on the right. Continue rightwards in a superb position, soon transferring to the upper of two breaks, to gain a heather ledge on the ridge crest. Surmount a small step to a heather ledge with block belays.

Heather scrambling within view of Bastow Gully leads to the foot of the next rock feature. The rib on the left is too difficult, and the central heather runnel topped by blocks too easy, so ascend a break diagonally to a ledge on the crest of the right-hand ridge. Now ascend the rib above, slightly on its left side (easier than it looks), to a blunt ridge.

Trend left over heather and boulders and, when practical, regain the left-hand rib. Ascend the rib with interest and some difficulty as close to the crest as possible, often overlooking Bastow Gully. If necessary, most of these difficulties can be avoided on the right. Continue to the large platform below the Nose on the North Ridge. Ascend to the summit as for Route 20.

Descent by this route: Not recommended.

Usual descents: As for Route 20.

Combinations: Refer to Route 10.

13: NOR' NOR' BUTTRESS VARIANT ** (3)

Similar to the Bastow route, though less successful in avoiding the gully it tries to escape. Suspect blocks on the entry pitch must be treated with respect. Exhilarating in the morning sunshine.

Summary: Difficult scrambling up discontinuous cracked ridges, with one gully diversion.

Conditions: The rock, lichenous through lack of traffic, is not as reliable as most on Tryfan (take special care at the blocks near the start). Dry conditions are essential. The buttress takes little drainage and faces the morning sun.

Approach: As for Route 12 to the foot of Bastow Gully. Beyond Bastow the Heather Terrace appears as a distinct gangway. Follow it to the next prominent gully, Nor' Nor', which is steeper than Bastow and contains more jammed boulders. One hour.

Ascent: From the entrance to Nor' Nor' Gully, scramble diagonally right over heathery rocks for 6m or so then ascend with difficulty over flaky blocks to heather ledges (15m total).

The next rise can be avoided scruffily on the right, though is best taken by one of two cracks near its left edge. To ascend the right-hand crack, surmount a flake on the right then thread a natural chock to protect a step-up into the crack. Continue to ledges and blocks below the next rise (12m).

Enter a gap behind perched blocks from the left and ascend the step slightly on the right. Continue up heather and short rises to below wrinkled rock of the next step. Take this on the right, returning to the crest as soon as practical. The ridge above rears up into rock climbing territory so escape easily left into Nor' Nor' Gully.

Ascend the right-hand side of the gully, initially over scree then by rock ribs and a couple of steps. At a vague fork, scrabble over a slabby boulder (if all else fails, try lying on the boulder facing outwards). Now for the clever bit, instead of plodding up the dirty gully, overcome a boulder on the right to enter the deep cleft and thus regain the buttress above its difficult section.

Scramble up the little rib above to gain the North Ridge flanking path. Ignore the block-filled remains of Nor' Nor' Gully and enjoy instead some excellent scrambling on the rib to its right. Finally pull through blocks on the left to arrive at the Notch at the top of Nor' Nor' Gully. Continue as for the North Ridge (Route 20) to the summit.

Descent by this route: Not recommended.

Usual descents: As for Route 20.

Combinations: Refer to Route 10.

14: NOR' NOR' GULLY (2/3)

Tolerable gully scrambling enlivened by several horrible obstacles, the most difficult of which is not easy to safeguard.

Summary: Unpleasant gully scrambling in a direct line from terrace to summit ridge.

Conditions: Lots of scree, not much water. The drier the better. Beware of stones dislodged by walkers crossing near the head of the gully.

Approach: As for Route 12 to the foot of Bastow Gully. Beyond Bastow the Heather Terrace appears as a distinct gangway. Follow it to the next prominent gully which is steeper than Bastow and contains more jammed boulders. One hour.

Ascent: Clamber over short steps and ascend the first main obstacle - a boulder blockage - by compact rock on the left. Take the second rise by rock and a vegetated groove on the right. Overcome the third rise on the left by an exposed and serious pitch on compact rock, stepping awkwardly left at the top to avoid a scree exit.

The gully now eases into a scree runnel with a few short steps. Where it curves right at a vague fork, scramble up 5m of mossy rocks and exit over a slabby boulder (if all else fails, try lying on the boulder and facing out to make best use of footholds). Scramble more easily up the gully continuation, emerging on the North Ridge at the prominent Notch. Continue as for Route 20 to the summit.

Descent by this route: Not recommended.

Usual descents: As for Route 20.

Combinations: Refer to Route 10.

15: NOR' NOR' GROOVE * (1/2)

A gully within a gully. Cleverly avoids all nasty obstacles in the true gully line by a series of devious leftward variants.

Summary: Quality scrambling up rock grooves followed by some heather and scree bashing to an easy gully exit.

Conditions: The grooves are on the shady side of the gully and so may remain greasy for a while after rain.

Approach: As for Route 12 to the foot of Bastow Gully. Beyond Bastow the Heather Terrace appears as a distinct gangway. Follow it to the next prominent gully, Nor' Nor', which is steeper than Bastow and contains more jammed boulders. One hour.

Ascent: From the entrance to Nor' Nor' Gully, ascend in five stages (with one awkward move - jammed right foot - to start the topmost shallow groove) a series of broken gully/grooves rising up its left side to enter a recess above the first major obstacle in the gully proper.

Ascend a hidden quartz slab on the left and bash up an open area of heather until crags loom above. Dodge back right - care with scree - to re-enter the gully above its evil third rise. Ascend the gully, here an easy scree runnel with a few short steps, to a vague fork within 15m of the difficult slabby boulder on Nor' Nor' Gully (refer to Route 14 if in doubt). Now either go 3m left and ascend a break, or avoid this section completely by taking the broad branch farther left, traversing back right at the North Ridge flanking path to regain the gully. Scramble up the gully continuation, over an initial step, to emerge on the North Ridge at the prominent Notch. Continue as for Route 20 to the summit.

Descent by this route: Not recommended without prior knowledge of the route in ascent.

Usual descents: As for Route 20.

Combinations: Refer to Route 10.

16: NORTH BUTTRESS VARIANT * (2)

Grass shelves and discontinuous rock ribs break up any continuity of line on the lower two-thirds of North Buttress. The upper third rears up in the compact crag of Terrace Wall, towering above the middle pastures. North Buttress rock climbs seek out difficulties in the lower ribs and then tackle Terrace Wall direct, whereas this route exploits the lower weaknesses and flanks Terrace Wall altogether. The line is devious but logical, winding through difficult terrain with surprising ease.

Summary: A rising right-to-left line across the face of a large, broken buttress, using runnels, ledges and rock grooves to avoid difficulties.

Conditions: Most of the easier-angled sections are covered in heather, though the protruding rock is clean and reliable. Worth waiting for dry weather. Faces the morning sun. On fine weekend days expect to encounter several parties of rock climbers following direct routes.

Approach: As for Route 12 to Bastow Gully. Beyond Bastow the terrace appears as a distinct gangway. Follow it, passing another prominent gully (Nor' Nor' Gully, steeper than Bastow and containing more jammed boulders), to the entrance to Green Gully, which has a grassy bed and no obvious continuation below the Heather Terrace. It defines the right-hand side of North Buttress. About 30m beyond Green Gully is a V-shaped recess, scree-covered at its base and backed by a runnel. It has a flake chimney on its right wall. One hour.

Ascent: The runnel behaves itself for 20m or so and then becomes unruly. Escape right here onto a broken rib and follow it, and its heather-covered continuation, to regain the runnel, which is grass-filled and easy. A couple of metres higher, exit left onto the main face by a ramp of heather and rock which terminates at a grass bower below a 10m bay wall. Ascend the wall, awkwardly at first and with a step left, to access easier ground in the centre of the face.

Continue to a level area beneath a wide, low wall turned easily on the left. Return right and avoid a second low wall by a ramp of slabs leading up left. Easy ground above the slabs again allows a return rightwards. The Terrace Wall - 50m of smooth, compact rock - now rises above. Avoid it by following a clean runnel which curves diagonally left beneath the wall and continues beyond as a series of steps. A final block-filled chimney gains the scree amphitheatre above North Gully.

The North Summit towers above on the right; reach it directly or follow the path which traverses the amphitheatre to gain the Central Summit high on the left.

Descent by this route: Not recommended.

Usual descents: As for Route 20.

Combinations: Refer to Route 10.

17: LITTLE AND NORTH GULLIES ** (1)

Central Buttress is the most massive of the three on the East Face and supports the summit blocks. Its base, furrowed by heather runnels and buttressed by rock ribs, presents a complicated structure on which potential lines are difficult to trace. This route uses the deep runnel of Little Gully to break through this lower barrier and thus gains the upper section of North Gully with few complications.

Summary: A pleasant introduction to gully scrambling via the bed of a dry, shallow trough and the easing upper part of a major fault line. Majestic surroundings.

Conditions: The rock is sound throughout with only a little scree debris, and that limited to the unimportant sections. A path over the grassy area is the result more of past traffic than present popularity.

Approach: As for Route 12 to Bastow Gully. Beyond Bastow the terrace appears as a distinct gangway. Follow it, passing another prominent gully (Nor' Nor' Gully, steeper than Bastow and containing more jammed boulders), to the entrance to Green Gully. This gully has a grassy bed and no obvious continuation below the Heather Terrace; it defines the right-hand side of North Buttress. Continue along the terrace to North Gully, which is deeper and more obviously difficult than its predecessors. It separates the North and Central buttresses. About 20m farther on a large block splits the terrace path. Face the cliff now and follow a subsidiary scree path rising left then right to a recess below walls and a short, square-cut gully. One hour fifteen minutes.

Ascent: Use a rock ramp on the outer left wall of the gully to avoid the mossy interior of the first step. Now ascend the trough - occasional rises of pleasant scrambling - to gain a notch overlooking

North Gully.

Continue up the trough a little on the left until it finally expires some distance short of North Gully. Follow a ledge which leads conveniently across to the right and thus, beyond a final rise, enter the scree bed of the main gully below unpleasant, moss-covered boulders.

A zig-zag on the right avoids the worst of the boulders and gains the scree terraces of the upper amphitheatre where a path will be found leading up left to the Central Summit.

Descent by this route: From the summit, follow the North Ridge flanking path to the amphitheatre between Central and North summits (where North Gully fans out). Descend the gully by scree ledges, avoiding boulders on the left (looking out), to a scree bay above a sinister drop. The ledge line which gains Little Gully will now be found at this level on the right (again looking out).

Usual descents: As for Route 20.

Combinations: Refer to Route 10.

18: SOUTH GULLY * (2 or 3)

High retaining walls restore a proper sense of enclosure to the wide recess of South Gully, the couloir which separates Central and South buttresses. There are no easy escapes once the initial barrier has been overcome.

Summary: Interesting scrambling over short steps - some of which are difficult - within a broad, largely scree-filled gully leading in a direct line to the summit.

Conditions: A fair amount of scree litters the bed, though the rock of the steeper sections is quite clean and sound. Beware of stones falling from above. The route carries surprisingly little drainage; however, the rock may remain greasy for a long time after wet weather.

Approach: As for Route 12 to Bastow Gully. Beyond Bastow the terrace appears as a distinct gangway. Follow it, passing another prominent gully (Nor' Nor' Gully, steeper than Bastow and containing more jammed boulders), to the entrance to Green Gully.

This gully has a grassy bed and no obvious continuation below the Heather Terrace; it defines the right-hand side of North Buttress. Continue along the terrace to North Gully, which is deeper and more obviously difficult than its predecessors. It separates the North and Central buttresses. About 20m farther on a large block splits the terrace path. Continue beyond it to the broad-based gully which separates Central and South buttresses. One hour fifteen minutes.

Ascent: The first step of the gully can be taken by a series of smooth and difficult grooves on the right, but it is far simpler to continue up the gully a short way then make a devious rightward traverse towards easy ground above the grooves. The gully bed now widens into a broad slope.

The left side gradually narrows into a scree chute then becomes rocky and is eventually barred; step left here and scramble up to easy ground. Beyond the scree, avoid a dividing rib by the short gully and steep slab just to its right.

Return to the main bed and surmount the final obstacle - a 10m dividing rib - by grooves on the right. An easy slope and short wall now lead to broken rocks between the Central and South summits.

Descent by this route: Take care to avoid the corner grooves near the foot of the gully: it is tempting to slide down the top groove, only to become trapped between a horribly insecure lower groove and an extremely difficult re-ascent.

Usual descents: As for Route 20.

Combinations: Refer to Route 10.

19: SOUTH BUTTRESS * (3)
This route, based on an intermittent rib line, takes the gentler left flank of South Buttress (when climbed direct throughout it is known in rock climbing guides as South Rib). Varied and pleasant, it shares many of the characteristics of East Face rock climbs - spiky ribs, heather runnels, and spacious ledges - yet receives comparatively little traffic.

The difficulties, though short and not excessive, are often exposed and therefore demand steadiness.

Summary: Ascends a series of delicate and exposed ribs then uses an easy chimney and a traversing ledge to gain the broken rocks of the South Summit.

Conditions: Takes little drainage and catches the sun from morning through mid-afternoon. Avoid in damp conditions.

Approach: As for Route 12 to Bastow Gully. Beyond Bastow the terrace appears as a distinct gangway. Follow it, passing another prominent gully (Nor' Nor' Gully, steeper than Bastow and containing more jammed boulders), to the entrance to Green Gully. This gully has a grassy bed and no obvious continuation below the Heather Terrace; it defines the right-hand side of North Buttress. Continue along the terrace to North Gully, which is deeper and more obviously difficult than its predecessors. It separates the North and Central buttresses. About 20m farther on a large block splits the terrace path. Continue beyond it to the broad-based South Gully which separates Central and South buttresses. A short distance beyond South Gully the terrace path divides; take the higher path for about 30m to a level slab of rock. A broken rib rises above the slab. One hour fifteen minutes.

Ascent: Follow the rib crest for about 50m until it degenerates into piled blocks. Now take the gangway which slants easily right towards the crest of a second rib. After a couple of metres on the gangway a broken chimney leads in 6m or so to a short, sloping ramp. Use the ramp to gain the rib and then follow its exposed crest to a notch.

The direct continuation of the rib above the notch is difficult so walk left for 15m to a chimney formed by huge perched blocks. Take the higher of two possible exits from the chimney and thus make an unlikely escape out to the right (facing the cliff) to regain the rib at a broad flat area.

Above, in the same line, is yet another rib. Scramble up the right edge then turn a blocking pillar on the right via a short chimney. Continue up the rib to a grass ledge below the final wall. Climb the wall directly by a short groove (hard to start but safe) or traverse scenically left to a platform near the South Ridge. Either way, easy rock then leads to the South Summit.

Descent by this route: Not recommended.

Usual descents: As for Route 20.

Combinations: Refer to Route 10.

20: NORTH RIDGE *** (1)

Tryfan's North Ridge is the most popular scramble in the Glyders. Its jagged crest, rising without deviation to the summit, can be seen from almost anywhere in the Ogwen Valley.

The ridge is broader than it seems and is more of a rocky shoulder than a true crest. Nevertheless the scrambling is always interesting, and when extended into a horseshoe ridge traverse (Route 10) provides one of the finest outings in North Wales.

Typically, short rises well-furnished with holds punctuate leisurely walking sections from where the unfolding view can be enjoyed to the full. Of numerous alternative lines, by far the best stay as close to the crest as possible.

Summary: Easy ridge scrambling from valley floor to summit. Impressive rock scenery.

Conditions: Extreme popularity means that holds are badly polished, though this does not detract from the enjoyment. Start early or late on fine weekend days to avoid crowds. Not especially difficult under wet or windy conditions, though it would be wise then to opt for the easier alternatives.

Approach: From Capel Curig or Bethesda along the A5. Park at a lay-by (GR:663 603) below the Milestone Buttress, a prominent feature on the lower west side of the North Ridge.

Ascent: From the lay-by, ascend near a stone wall then trend left before reaching the Milestone Buttress to gain a shoulder on the North Ridge. Ascend a boulder slope and break through a short barrier at its top. Continue slightly on the left side of the broad ridge to a quartz platform (the Cannon, a famous rock feature, will be found over on the right).

Surmount the next high barrier near its left side (though not too far left or you'll miss an entertaining scramble) and continue to another large platform below a prominent nose of rock. Take time

59

West Face of Tryfan

The Cannon, North Ridge of Tryfan (Route 20)

to inspect this barrier for the best line then follow it on polished rock to a minor summit, descending on the far side to the Notch (or avoid the nose by traversing its left side to the Notch).

Escape the Notch by trending right - not difficult - and ascend a gully to the North Summit. Continue easily over boulders to the twin standing stones of Adam and Eve on the Central Summit.

Descent by this route: In descent it is worth following the path which flanks the North Ridge on its east side. Gain this from the summit via a prominent slab on the east side of Adam and Eve (or by other means). The path skirts the amphitheatres of the upper East Face, though rarely drops more than 30m or so below the crest.

Usual descents: (i) Via Cwm Bochlwyd. Traverse to the South Summit then descend the South Ridge, generally by its gentler west side, to the broad col between South and Far South summits. Again avoid difficulties by flanking the Far South Summit on the west side and then descend to Bwlch Tryfan (GR:662 588). Turn right and follow an improving path down to the Llyn Bochlwyd outflow. Descend the path on the west bank of the stream then cross it for a rightward diagonal descent over boggy ground to gain the A5 at a large car park (GR:659 601) less than 500m from the start. (ii) Via the Heather Terrace. Descend the South Ridge to a prominent col. Cross the wall on the left by a stile and begin descending a depression on the east side of the mountain. The terrace is surprisingly difficult to locate so look carefully for signs of the path on the left (looking out). Follow the terrace across the East Face to the level area above the eroded scree gully of the approach to Route 12.

Combinations: Refer to Route 10.

21: MILESTONE BUTTRESS APPROACH *** (3)

The Milestone Buttress is the most prominent and accessible crag on the West Face. Facing the afternoon sun, its blocky front - free of vegetation and shaped by cracks, chimneys and slabs - makes an exciting approach to the North Ridge, avoiding the rather plodding nature of the earlier part of the normal route.

Because this is the easiest way up the buttress, careful route-finding is essential. Roped protection should be considered for some of the more awkward and exposed obstacles.

Summary: A rising diagonal line - occasionally difficult and exposed - across an open, slabby buttress.

Conditions: The rock is reliable but badly polished where the line crosses parts of rock climbs. It becomes slippery when wet and the route is then best avoided.

Approach: From Capel Curig or Bethesda along the A5. Park at a lay-by (GR:663 603) below the Milestone Buttress, a prominent feature on the lower west side of the North Ridge. From the lay-by, ascend near a stone wall - soon crossing it at a stile - then clamber across boulders trending right to below the slabby west face of the buttress. Twenty minutes.

Ascent: A protruding narrow slab defines the right-hand side of the main slab frontage, beyond which is an open scree couloir (Milestone Gully - Route 22). Climb the slab in two stages of 8m - intermediate belay if required - on good but polished and occasionally spaced holds. Alternatively, avoid the slab by traversing in from the gully at one of several points. Now scramble more easily for 10m to a recess beneath the huge tilted block of the Pulpit.

Crouch left beneath the Pulpit and follow a diagonal line of flakes leftwards to a recessed ledge. Swing up to the left - exposed - and continue diagonally left, across wrinkled slabs, to another recess. Go up over blocks to enter a large, rock-walled bay.

The corner chimney is too difficult so ascend an easier one 4m to the right on spiky holds to grass in 7m. (From here it is possible to traverse right across easy-angled slabs to enter the Milestone Gully just below its baffling step.) Move left to enter a rock trough and ascend this to open heather slopes. Finally, trend right to arrive at boulders at the top of Milestone Gully.

Descent by this route: Not as difficult as you might expect, though certainly not recommended without thorough knowledge of the route in ascent.

Usual descents: As for Route 20. To return directly to the foot of the

Ascending Glyder Fach via Bristly Ridge, (Route 27)

face, descend via Route 22.

Combinations: Though possible to gain the North Ridge (Route 20) directly up heather and boulder slopes, it is best to maintain the character and difficulty of this approach by combining it with Route 23.

22: MILESTONE GULLY APPROACH ** (1/2)

An ugly-looking gully which in fact provides 50m of excellent scrambling. The difficulties are sustained but not excessive, apart from one avoidable step.

Summary: A short approach gully, damp but entertaining.

Conditions: Wet conditions are normal. The heavily polished and water-worn rock is free from lichen and so loss of friction in such conditions is minimal. The rock is of better quality than that usually found in gullies.

Approach: As for Route 21. An open scree couloir defines the right-hand side of the buttress front. Twenty minutes.

Ascent: Ascend the couloir into the narrowing gully then trend left up wet rock shelves. A smooth, chin-high shelf bars the return back right. Use whatever means you have at your disposal to overcome it (or avoid it by taking a rightward line from below the wet shelves), then scramble up the cracked left side of the upper rock slot. Exit left at the top over blocks.

Descent by this route: In exact reverse of the ascent, and noticeably more difficult.

Usual descents: From the summit of Tryfan, as for Route 20. There is no simple direct descent to the foot of the gully so it is best to ascend trending left to gain the North Ridge and then descend the lower section of that route.

Combinations: Ascend direct over heather and boulders to gain the North Ridge (Route 20) or follow Route 23.

Creeping up the Cat-walk on the Chasm Face (Route 28)

23: MILESTONE CONTINUATION ** (3)

A worthwhile diversion for those approaching the North Ridge via the Milestone Buttress, with scrambling of similar style and difficulty.

Summary: 40m of difficult but protectable scrambling up the cracks and ribs of a continuation buttress.

Conditions: Unlike the Milestone, the buttress is rarely visited. Consequently there is more vegetation but less polish. Must be dry. Catches the afternoon sun.

Approach: Initially by ascending Route 21 or 22. From the top of Milestone Gully, walk up 30m to the base of a second crag, a Milestone Buttress in miniature.

Ascent: Start at the toe of the buttress and climb a hand-width dog-leg crack for 10m to a ledge on the left edge of the slab (possible belay here, and if needed an escape down to the left). Make a long reach onto a second ledge and scramble awkwardly up a series of easing ribs until they are swallowed by the heather slope. Continue on rock near the left edge or, more easily, up heather on the right. Easy scrambling directly ahead gains the North Ridge. Continue as for Route 20 to the summit.

Descent by this route: Not recommended.

Usual descents: As for Route 20.

Combinations: Refer to Route 10.

24: WRINKLED TOWER *** (3)

Beyond the busy Milestone Buttress the West Face promises a great scrambling adventure - provided a route can be contrived among the clinging heather, cascading runnels and impossible towers. This is that route. The audacious solution to the Faulty Tower lies at the upper limit of scrambling difficulty, though this and other obstacles can be adequately protected with a rope and a few runners.

Summary: Varied and difficult scrambling up a series of intimidating steps and towers on the huge West Face of Tryfan.

Conditions: Unfrequented and so expect lichenous rock. This gives

Milestone Buttress approach routes to the North Ridge of Tryfan

good friction when dry but is hopelessly greasy when wet. Wait for a dry period. Faces the afternoon sun.

Approach: Initially as for Route 21. Beyond the Milestone Gully a second, vegetated buttress is bounded on the right by a watercourse, to the right of which are acres of heather-covered slabs. Walk beneath the slabs and enter the scree couloir which defines their right-hand side, below a bristling rib. Thirty minutes.

Ascent: From the couloir entrance, ascend leftwards on heather and rough slabs. Gain piled blocks several metres above either by a through route on the left or, better, by a slabby corner on the right.

Continue more easily then move left to piled rocks on the rib crest below a smooth nose of rock.

Gain a small ledge at 2m then use a perfect flake to go out left, high or low, to a useful spike (runner). Climb straight above the spike on good holds, finishing with a difficult move - avoidable by a step left to grass - to huge blocks. (10m)

Scramble over the blocks and pull through a gap on the left to gain a large ledge at the left side of a 4m pinnacle flake. A broad, slabby rib rises above; ascend it slightly on the left via blocks until the angle relents. Scramble easily up a gently angled shallow rib of blocks until beneath the left side of the imposing Faulty Tower set above distinctive daubs of quartz.

From the top of the rib, traverse right for 10m or so to the foot of the improbable tower. A chimney fault on the left, partially choked by a 5m flake, offers a slim chance. Struggle up the chimney (thread runner) to a recess in its upper part. The slimy continuation is appallingly insecure, so, unlikely as it may seem, get onto a ledge on the left and follow a narrowing, sloping ramp leftwards into a position of stomach-turning exposure. Keep your nerve and reach for a flake on the very edge (sling protection). Now stretch high above the flake to a superb edge and pull over onto a ledge. Block belay a little higher. If all this sounds too exciting it can be avoided on the left by scrambling easily above the shallow rib then traversing rightwards to the block belay.

The next task is to regain the crest of the tower. Either gain it directly above the block with long reaches to flakes, or sidle a few metres left and climb the deep rift behind a flake pinnacle, stepping out (exposed) to easy ground above.

Ten metres of easy scrambling lead to the base of a clean slab split by a boot-wide crack. Ascend the crack and flake slivers to the slab top in 10m (avoidable, but it's a pity to miss this superb pitch). Continue up easing rock and scramble up a final rib via shattered blocks and a slab near the left edge. Ascend over heather and boulders to gain the North Ridge about 100m above the Cannon. Continue to the summit as for Route 20.

Descent by this route: Not recommended.

Usual descents: As for Route 20.

Combinations: Refer to Route 10.

25: WEST FACE ROUTE * (2 or 3)

A scruffier alternative to the Wrinkled Tower, following an interrupted line of slabs, ribs and towers on the huge West Face. Less technical than the Wrinkled Tower, though not as easy to protect.

Summary: Varied scrambling - good to start and finish - up a large, broken face.

Conditions: The start is water-washed in bad weather but dry otherwise. Beyond the start the rock is lichenous and so dry conditions are desirable. Some rock is of doubtful quality. Faces the afternoon sun.

Approach: Initially as for Route 24. Right of the scree couloir is a less prominent rib, and to the right of this a scree tongue leading into a runnel of heather and rock. Farther right is a broad rock rib, below which is a ledge of grass and scree. Thirty minutes.

Ascent: The left side of the rib is uninviting so start at the right side of the ledge, almost in the corner formed by a protruding rib.

Scramble up clean rock, slightly left at first then straight up (easier than it looks). After 50m or so, ignore easy ground on the right and trend left onto a rib of rock and heather, ascending this and the blocks beyond until barred by a smooth slab.

Ascend the slab by a central heather trough until it ends after about 7m, then escape diagonally left via spikes to heather.

The next step may be overcome in one of two ways, both of them rather precarious: (i) Clamber over poised blocks on the left side, or, if this does not appeal (and it may well not), (ii) ascend a narrowing grass tongue on the right then traverse high or low below two rift exits to gain the left edge. Now pull convincingly over blocks and traverse the left wall to enter the left-hand line above its most unstable blocks. (Grade 3)

Exit awkwardly and continue to a 6m barrier climbed centrally or avoided to left or right. Now take any route to the terminal Sunset Rib and climb it on superb rock with a difficult finale to arrive on the North Ridge at the large platform below the Nose. Continue to the summit as for Route 20.

Descent by this route: Not recommended.

Usual descents: As for Route 20.

Combinations: Refer to Route 10.

26: SOUTH RIDGE DIRECT ** (1)

A shorter, easier and sunnier version of the North Ridge. It barely warrants a description but it is worth noting as a suitable introduction to scrambling.

Summary: Easy scrambling on avoidable steps to a magnificent rocky summit.

Conditions: Exposed to bad weather and strong cross winds, though not dangerously so. Takes no drainage and dries very quickly after rain.

Approach: As for Route 27 to Bwlch Tryfan. One hour thirty minutes.

Ascent: Ignore easier options on the left and instead ascend the broad-backed ridge directly over the Far South and South summits to the twin standing stones of Adam and Eve on the Central Summit, seeking or avoiding difficulties at will.

Descent by this route: A suitable descent, though some steps are difficult to see from above - be prepared to search around for a feasible line.

Usual descents: As for Route 20.

GLYDER FACH (990m)

Though Glyder Fach's summit plateau cannot match the fairytale loftiness of Tryfan, it lacks nothing in dramatic setting and outlook. Some 100m east of the summit, where huge monoliths lay scattered like giant matchsticks spilled from a box, you will find the Cantilever, improbably balanced on its supporting rock, tempting you to pose photogenically at its tip; and 300m south-west, the stockade of massive splinters known as Castell y Gwynt - Castle of the Winds.

The remote north-west face hangs in a complex mural of crags and boulder slopes above Cwm Bochlwyd, cold and unfriendly on grim winter days, warm and welcoming on bright summer afternoons. Concentrated on these crudely sculptured rocks are some of the best scrambles in North Wales. The face is bounded to the east by Bristly Ridge and to the west by the Gribin Ridge. Both are good: Bristly Ridge is described in this section, while the Gribin Ridge is more logically described with the Glyder Fawr routes.

27: BRISTLY RIDGE *** (1)
This famous and aptly named ridge defines the left side of the north-west face and links Bwlch Tryfan with the Glyder Fach summit plateau. Though worthwhile in its own right, an ascent of this remotely situated and exhilarating scramble makes a natural and logical continuation to a traverse of Tryfan by its North and South ridges (Route 10).

Of many alternative lines on the flanks of the broad ridge, a direct route is nowhere excessively difficult and proves to be the most satisfying.

Summary: Straightforward scrambling on a rocky and pinnacled ridge.

Conditions: The polished rock is mostly sound, but take care with poor material near the start. Suffers little drainage and so dries quickly after rain during warm or breezy weather. Unpleasant though not especially difficult when wet. Vulnerable to strong cross winds. Extremely popular during fine summer weekends; start early or late to avoid crowds.

Approach: From Capel Curig or Bethesda along the A5 to a car park at Ogwen Cottage (GR:649 604), or use overspill parking in lay-bys farther east. Take the path behind the toilet block, fork left after a few metres, and cross a stile and footbridge onto the stone track. Where the track curves rightwards towards Cwm Idwal, bear left over marshy ground and ascend a steep path on the west bank of a stream to Llyn Bochlwyd. Cross the stream outflow and follow the path to Bwlch Tryfan (GR:662 588). One hour thirty minutes.

Ascent: Follow the stone wall to the base of Bristly Ridge, the obvious pinnacled buttress leading up towards the summit of Glyder Fach. From the foot of the lowest crags, go 10m right and ascend a short gully, exiting left over a man-made wall to the foot of the more imposing Sinister Gully. Scramble carefully up its bed, detouring onto the left wall where it steepens, to easier ground.

Continue up a slabby shoulder to a narrowing of the ridge. Scramble over a small pinnacle onto a larger one then descend into the prominent notch of Great Pinnacle Gap. Escape by a short wall just right of the slender Great Pinnacle, then pass through a gap between a squat pinnacle (on the right) and the main body of the ridge to reach easier ground. An elevated boulder pavement finally leads onto the summit plateau.

Walk south-west to join the normal ascent path and follow it (with a slight detour left to see the Cantilever) to the summit rock pile.

Descent by this route: The ridge makes an interesting descent to Bwlch Tryfan, though prior knowledge of the route will help in avoiding false lines, particularly in the lower reaches.

Usual descents: (i) The eroded scree couloir east of Bristly Ridge provides a fast if scruffy descent to Bwlch Tryfan. (ii) From the summit, descend the east shoulder over boulders then grass to within a few hundred metres of Llyn y Caseg-fraith then turn sharp left to follow the mostly contouring Miners' Track north-west to Bwlch Tryfan. (iii) From the summit, continue south-west - scrambling around or over Castell y Gwynt - to Bwlch y Ddwy Glyder. Ignore the continuation of the path to Glyder Fawr and instead circle the rim of Cwm Bochlwyd onto the promontory above the Gribin Ridge and descend this (Route 34) via Llyn Bochlwyd to Ogwen Cottage. (iv) From Bwlch y Ddwy Glyder (GR:652 582), descend directly into Cwm Bochlwyd. This is more useful as an alternative descent from routes on the north-west face.

Combinations: Refer to Route 10.

28: THE CHASM FACE *** (3)

The most impressive of the sharp-edged columns of rock which protrude from the north-west face of Glyder Fach are clustered above and to the left of the Alphabet Slab, a distinctive feature at the foot of the cliffs. It is through these sentinels that the Chasm Face route finds its way.

Uniquely improbable in the lower part, where it weaves and tunnels through vertical rock, its upper slope entertains with open scrambling on superb rock.

Summary: Varied scrambling up walls and ramps into a trap escaped by a hole in the wall. Pleasant scrambling over short steps on the upper face leads to the summit.

Conditions: Clean, sound rock but polished on the flake wall and cat-walk. Dries relatively quickly on breezy summer days, but not otherwise. Best enjoyed in the afternoon sun in summer. Parts of the route are shared with The Chasm rock climb, so expect company on fine summer weekends.

Approach: As for Route 27 to Llyn Bochlwyd. From the far side of the lake, a vague path leads up heather and boulder slopes to the lowest point of the cliffs. Ascend a scree gully on the left side of the Alphabet Slab to a ledge above. The blunt base of Main Gully Ridge rises above, and to its left the shallow depression of Main Gully. One hour fifteen minutes.

Ascent: Scramble up Main Gully for about 40m, until above the chockstone step, then trend left over grass ledges. Pass above the wide slot of the Chasm itself and struggle over piled blocks (protectable) to gain a 2m by 3m triangular ledge below a loathsome corner.

The corner looks hopeless, so climb up just to its left for 3m then make a series of diagonal ape-like swings on flakes and spikes (protection) to a belay in a notch on the left edge. (6m)

From the notch, creep up a half-metre wide cat-walk - exposed but not difficult - to enter the upper chasm. Overcome a smooth step and go up to beneath an arch formed by a fallen block (claustrophobic, overweight or overclad scramblers use this arch - the Arch Tempter - to escape rightwards into Main Gully). (8m)

Above the arch the dreaded Vertical Vice - crux of The Chasm rock climb - threatens all sorts of unspeakable torture, so avoid this insecure chimney/crack by wriggling up the first part of the chimney then squirming through a narrow cleft to enter the bowels of the mountain. A vertical chimney completes this Subterranean Exit to daylight.

The main difficulties are now over, so find your own way up or around the outcrops of the upper slope. Depending on the line chosen, you will arrive on the summit plateau somewhere between the Cantilever and the summit rock pile.

Descent by this route: Not recommended.

Usual descents: As for Route 27. For those wishing to return directly to the foot of the face after completing only the technical section, traverse right and descend Main Gully (Route 29) to the top of the Alphabet Slab.

29: MAIN GULLY ** (1)

A gloomy scramble of surprising quality. It is not really a gully at all, but a rocky depression between the columns of the Chasm Face area and the protruding bulk of Main Gully Ridge.

Summary: Simple scrambling up a rocky depression followed by avoidable problems on the short steps of the upper face.

Conditions: The rock is unexpectedly clean and sound. Neither grass nor rock debris intrudes. Dries more quickly than most gullies, especially on breezy summer days, but remains damp and greasy otherwise.

Approach: As for Route 28.

Ascent: Move left from the top of the Alphabet Slab to enter the depression and ascend to a narrowing at a slot (30m). Continue for 7m then overcome a chockstone, easiest on the left, to a region of grass ledges.

Ascend more easily to the upper section and scramble up this, sustained at a gentle standard, to emerge near the top of Main Gully Ridge.

Trend left to gain the slope above the Chasm Face and scramble over or around short steps to the summit plateau.

Descent by this route: A practical means of descent from neighbouring scrambles - provided it can be found. Hardest at the chockstone near the bottom.

Usual descents: As for Route 27.

30: MAIN GULLY RIDGE *** (2 or 3)

A blunt ridge above the Alphabet Slab provides the most direct means of ascending the Main Cliff. The scrambling is exposed and technical, though at least the hard start can be avoided if necessary. Spike belays will be found at intervals.

Summary: Airy climbing up walls and ribs followed by easier scrambling up the broken upper face.

Conditions: Takes little drainage but vegetation retards drying. Best on a warm, dry afternoon. Excellent rock.

Approach: As for Route 28.

Ascent: From spikes at the foot of the ridge, balance diagonally right high or low (the latter being easier and more secure) to gain easier rock and hence a block on the ridge crest (9m). Alternatively (reducing the overall grade to 2), ascend Main Gully for 6m or so then traverse right past three spikes and pull into a position of

North-West Face of Glyder Fach

32

33

sudden exposure at the block on the ridge crest.

Pull awkwardly onto a higher block and go up to a grass recess below a corner. Ignore the corner and step right onto a rib, ascending this to another ledge. (7m)

Once again ignore the corner above and move right to ascend the rib for 5m or so to a level section on the crest, about 40m above the top of the Alphabet Slab.

The ridge above is too difficult so either scramble up the slot to its right, or trend right for 10m to gain East Gully Ridge at the notch of piled blocks and ascend this (Grade 3).

Continue up easing rock above the merged ridges then trend left to finish up the pleasant upper section of the Chasm Face.

Descent by this route: Not recommended.

Usual descents: As for Route 28. For those wishing to return directly to the foot of the face after completing only the technical section, traverse left into Main Gully (Route 29) from the uppermost rib and descend this to the top of the Alphabet Slab.

31: EAST GULLY RIDGE *** (2 or 3)

The ridge overlooking East Gully also makes an unlikely scramble. In this case the difficult lower section is completely avoided by a long traverse from above the Alphabet Slab, while the intricacies of the middle section can, if necessary, be flanked on the gully side - though none too easily. Belays can be found at intervals.

Summary: Difficult scrambling up a series of ribs leads to easier scrambling on the upper face.

Conditions: Takes little drainage but vegetation retards drying. Best on a warm, dry afternoon. Excellent rock.

Approach: Initially as for Route 28. From the top of the Alphabet Slab, follow a narrow path rightwards, crossing the slabby rock of a protruding rib, then gradually descend rightwards to a sloping rock ledge at the foot of the left-bounding ridge of East Gully. This is about 50m from the top of the Alphabet Slab.

Ascent: Take the initial rise on the right edge (excellent friction), or avoid it to the left or right, to a prominent notch below a narrower rib. Follow excellent holds for 30m to a level area then scramble over blocks for 10m to a notch of piled blocks below a more compact section of the ridge.

Scramble up a few metres then climb a 2m hand-width crack, mantelshelving onto a spike at its top (runner). Now step delicately up to the left and go up a few metres to a narrow rock ledge - difficult but protected. Alternatively, go 3m right from the notch to a bilberry ledge, up a slab for 3m to blocks, pull strenuously up a crack on the left to a ledge, and then gain the narrow ledge of the direct route by a simple corner. Continue up easing rock to block belays in 5m, just short of another notch.

The Main and East Gully ridges merge above; ascend the right-hand edge, easing, until it narrows and curves left. Continue trending left to gain pleasant scrambling on the upper part of the Chasm Face.

Descent by this route: Not recommended.

Usual descents: As for Route 28. For those wishing to return directly to the foot of the face after completing only the technical section, traverse left into Main Gully (Route 29) from the uppermost rib and descend this to the top of the Alphabet Slab.

32: SHARK BUTTRESS *** (3)

This wandering line seeks out the best from the central area of terraced buttresses. Complex route-finding and surprising escapes add to the anxiety and interest.

Summary: Varied and difficult scrambling up a huge face studded with outcrops.

Conditions: Much the least popular part of Main Cliff. Wait for dry conditions. Generally excellent rock but with some suspect seams and loose blocks.

Approach: As for Route 31 to a sloping rock ledge at the foot of the left-bounding ridge of East Gully. Cross the gully to a grassy shoulder below a compact, vertical tower supported on wrinkly slabs (Hawk's Nest Buttress). One hour fifteen minutes.

Ascent: Ascend diagonally right across the lower slabs (not difficult

Cresting the buttress on Dolmen Ridge (Route 33)

but exposed and unprotected), passing above a narrow chimney, to grass ledges at the right-hand side of the buttress. (25m)

Scramble over blocks for 6m to a notch behind a large flake. Step from the flake onto a smooth, slabby wall and climb it to grass ledges in 3m. Ascend the left side of the recess into a shallow slot. After a few metres this steepens and becomes vegetated so pull out left onto a tiny ledge below a wide crack. Ascend the crack to a block on the right then reach left on a good flake-edged block to pull out onto the buttress front.

Ascend left over piled blocks until below a huge pinnacle with a chockstone jammed near its top. To the right is a smooth-cornered recess: ascend the wide left-hand crack for 2m to spikes, fix thread protection, then pull energetically onto the left edge. Continue up wrinkly slabs for 3m or so to block belays.

Shark Pinnacle stands 10m above, its summit an idyllic viewpoint in the evening sunlight. But it will not be gained easily. Either pull through the jaws right of the wedged block on the valley side, or climb delicately up its 5m back on the mountain side. Descend by a controlled slither.

Scramble up behind the pinnacle and avoid a step via the grass recess and dirty corner on the left. Cross over the rib on the right (15m above the Shark) and go up to a grass belvedere. Continue for a few metres over slabs and a rock glacis then go left up a grass terrace to below Perch Pinnacle. Ascend steep rock then escape rightwards below the pinnacle itself.

Excellent, easier scrambling above leads on to Dolmen Ridge just before it dips to the col and merges into the main bulk of the mountain.

Descent by this route: Not recommended.

Usual descents: As for Route 27.

33: DOLMEN RIDGE *** (3)

The curving line of Central Gully defines the right-hand side of the huge face taken by Shark Buttress. On the left side of the gully, at about half height, stands the compact, triangular crag of Dolmen Buttress. This excellent scramble crosses Central Gully to ascend the upper right edge of Dolmen Buttress, then uses the left-bounding ridge of the gully to gain the Glyder Fach plateau just a few metres from the summit rock pile.

Summary: Awkward problems on the short steps of an introductory buttress followed by a steep pitch on a compact buttress. Less difficult scrambling along a curving ridge leads to the summit.

Conditions: The rock is generally rough and sound. Takes little drainage but wait for warm, dry conditions. Catches the late afternoon sun in summer.

Approach: As for Route 27 to Llyn Bochlwyd. From the far side of the lake, ascend towards the back of the cwm (ie. heading for Bwlch y Ddwy Glyder, the col between Castell y Gwynt and the Gribin Ridge) to a tiny pool - marked only on 1:25,000 maps - below the large, central buttress of the north-west face. Central Gully is now obvious: a wide, shallow rift running almost the full height of the cliffs. One hour fifteen minutes.

Ascent: Ascend the large buttress right of Central Gully by an intricate, right-to-left slanting line to a scree-covered shoulder level with the foot of Dolmen Buttress. Traverse across the gully just below a narrowing and ascend an easy ramp to gain the crest of Dolmen Buttress at about half height (alternative means of approaching this point include the gully itself - unpleasant - and the rocks to its left).

From the end of the ramp, ascend a short groove and its left edge (spike) to an easy but exposed step left round the arête. Scramble diagonally left to gain the main ridge crest.

The ridge now eases but continues to give interesting scrambling in exposed positions overlooking Central Gully. Eventually it curves to the right, dips to a small col, and then merges into the main bulk of the mountain. The summit lies directly ahead.

Descent by this route: Not recommended.

Usual descents: As for Route 27.

GLYDER FAWR (999m)

Glyder Fawr occupies a commanding position at the bend in the centre of the 15km main Glyders ridge. Its Cwm Idwal face rises in a series of slabs and walls almost from lakeside to summit - a vertical height difference of almost 500m. This is the most interesting and best known face of the mountain, not least because of its supporting plinth known as the Idwal Slabs, a traditional rock climbing venue and the most distinctive landmark in Cwm Idwal. Less obvious challenges await in Cwm Cneifion, a hanging valley enclosed by Glyder Fawr and its subsidiary ridge of the Gribin, and on the southern flank which rises dramatically out of the Llanberis Pass defile.

The most popular walking route to the summit begins from Ogwen Cottage and ascends via Cwm Idwal and the Devil's Kitchen, culminating in a demoralising slog up the scree paths above Llyn y Cwn (the lake can also be reached from the west by a good path from Gwastadnant in the Llanberis Pass). It can also be gained via the south spur, starting from Pen y Pass. Otherwise the peak is generally combined with an ascent of Glyder Fach in a circular walk from Pen y Pass or Ogwen Cottage.

Scrambling interest focuses on the northern side; on the north-west (Idwal) face, and on the ridges which bound or lie within Cwm Cneifion. The final route in this section ascends out of the Llanberis Pass via Esgair Felen, the south-west spur.

34: GRIBIN RIDGE * (1)

The Gribin rises between Cwm Bochlwyd and Cwm Cneifion to join the main Glyders ridge midway between Glyder Fach and Glyder Fawr. A popular, scrambly walk, it provides a pleasant route up to, or down from, either of the two summits. Impressive views into the bordering cwms compensate for the trifling amount of genuine scrambling.

The usual route on the upper rockier section flanks the crest of the Cneifion side, so take this section direct to avoid other parties, increase scrambling interest, and restore concentration with a

83

sobering exposure to the drop into Cwm Bochlwyd.

Summary: Enjoyable walking along a prominent, easy-angled ridge enlivened by some straightforward scrambling on a final rock crest.

Conditions: Not greatly affected by wet rock, though exposed to cross-winds. In either case it may be best to follow the easier and more sheltered normal line slightly on the Cwm Cneifion flank of the upper rock crest.

Approach: Via the A5 from Capel Curig or Bethesda. Park at Ogwen Cottage (GR:649 604), or at overspill parking areas to the east. Follow the Cwm Idwal path until it curves right. Bear left here, using stepping-stones to cross a boggy area, then ascend the eroded stream bank to Llyn Bochlwyd. Turn right and follow a path onto the right-bounding ridge of Cwm Bochlwyd. Forty minutes.

Ascent: Once gained, the ridge path is well worn and obvious. Apart from an occasional short step it involves nothing more than pleasant walking to a large grass shoulder below the upper rock crest. (The False Gribin, Route 35, and Cneifion Arête, Route 36, emerge near here from east and west respectively.)

Above, the ridge rears up, narrows and turns to rock. The normal path zig-zags up this section on the Cneifion (west) side, though for maximum interest it should be taken direct. The crest soon falls back into a stone-studded slope with the paths to Glyder Fach (east) and Glyder Fawr (west) nearby.

Descent by this route: A descent of the Gribin is quite feasible. When approaching from Glyder Fawr in mist, contour the rim of Cwm Cneifion to be certain of locating the promontory at the top of the upper rock crest. On the lower section, stay on the right (east) flank to be sure of finding the path which leads across to the Llyn Bochlwyd outflow.

Usual descents: From the summit of Glyder Fawr, descend as for Route 38. Refer to the previous section for descents from Glyder Fach.

Combinations: Perhaps the best use of the Gribin is as a descent from Glyder Fach, after an ascent via Tryfan and Bristly Ridge, as the final part of the Bochlwyd Horseshoe (Route 10).

35: FALSE GRIBIN * (1)

A variant on the Gribin which, by judicious choice of line, can treble the amount of scrambling. The name is a little unfair because, although the ridge is a subsidiary one, it is the true continuation of the upper rock crest. Though not often ascended, it bears the marks of the occasional, and probably inadvertent, descent.

Summary: A scrambling approach up a broad-backed subsidiary ridge to the final rock crest of the Gribin.

Conditions: In general as for Route 34. Being less used, the rocks are rather more vegetated and lichenous than those on the Gribin and therefore the ascent requires extra care during wet weather.

Approach: Initially as for Route 34 to Llyn Bochlwyd. Circle the lake to its south-west shore and ascend to the indistinct foot of the ridge. Forty minutes.

Ascent: Ascend first over rock and heather on the broad-backed lower ridge. Not much scrambling here, but soon the ridge steepens to give good, easy scrambling with a wide choice of line.

The route joins the Gribin Ridge just above the grass shoulder. Continue as for Route 34.

Descent by this route: The route is not significantly more difficult in descent.

Usual descents: From the summit of Glyder Fawr, descend as for Route 38. Refer to the previous section for descents from Glyder Fach.

Combinations: As for Route 34.

36: CNEIFION ARÊTE ** (3)

Cwm Cneifion, high and remote, nestles between Glyder Fawr and the upper part of the Gribin. Clogwyn Du looms impressively from the shady side of the cwm yet offers the scrambler nothing more than inferior possibilities on flanking rocks. In contrast, the sunnier Gribin side of the cwm appears to provide limitless opportunities. Unfortunately, a large part of this face consists of scree-littered and nondescript slabby rock. For this reason the selected scrambles follow only the more continuous ribbons of rock, of which the

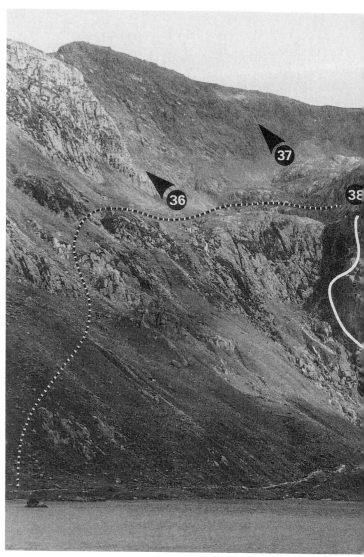

Idwal Face of Glyder Fawr and Cwm Cneifion approaches

Cneifion Arête is by far the most distinct.

The initial 30m rise of the arête could be classed as easy rock climbing rather than scrambling, though it can be protected with a couple of sling runners. The easier upper part provides scrambling of a sustained and exposed nature which can be climbed in pitches, 'moving together' or solo according to conditions and the experience of the party.

Summary: A choice of approaches to a remote cwm escaped via exposed and initially difficult scrambling on a sharp rock arête.

Conditions: West-facing and takes little drainage. Rock quality is generally good. Square-cut holds allow an ascent in wet conditions, though the increase in difficulty soon becomes unacceptable if these are combined with strong winds. The arête is relatively popular, though sufficiently remote for it to be spared overcrowding.

Approach: As for Route 38 into lower Cwm Cneifion. The arête now appears above on the left, knife-edged and obvious (refer to *Combinations* for other approaches). One hour.

Ascent: A slabby and vegetated front is bounded on the right by a near-vertical side wall; the route ascends the easier lower part of this wall to gain the crest between wall and slab, which it then follows as closely as possible.

A scree path rises steeply to a small bay just right of the foot of the arête proper. From the bay, 10m of steep climbing on good holds leads to a runner (or belay) just below the crest. Traverse awkwardly right for a few metres then ascend leftwards to gain the crest below a short, sandy chimney (belay). The chimney leads to easier ground within a few metres.

Now that the major difficulties are over, the best line follows the exposed crest as closely as possible. This can become a little too exciting during windy conditions, though numerous spike belays are available if required.

The arête finally falls back into the Gribin Ridge at the large grass shoulder below its final rock nose. Continue as for Route 34.

Descent by this route: Not recommended.

Usual descents: As for Route 38. It is possible to descend into upper

Cwm Cneifion via the stony ribs and runnels at its head, though this is not recommended except as a quick approach to the foot of Maybe Tower Rib (Route 37).

Combinations: Normal approaches to the arête are tedious so consider gaining Seniors' Ridge via Route 39 or 40 and contouring left into lower Cwm Cneifion.

37: MAYBE TOWER RIB * (2/3)
To the right of Cneifion Arête the Gribin flank of Cwm Cneifion curves round in a shattered headwall containing much rock but few distinctive features. Though short and scruffy compared to Cneifion Arête, the rib has its moments and the solitude will be appreciated by seasoned scramblers.

Difficulties on the Tower are short but appreciable; belays and protection are available at intervals throughout this section.

Summary: A choice of long approaches to the upper bowl of a remote cwm escaped by awkward scrambling on a protruding rib.

Conditions: The rib takes little drainage but is often damp and cold due to its north-westerly aspect and high altitude (850m). Wet lichen adds to the insecurity in other than perfectly dry conditions. The rock is reasonably sound, though the piled blocks near the top should be handled with care.

Approach: As for Route 38 to lower Cwm Cneifion then continue into the upper cwm. One hour thirty minutes by the quickest approach.

Ascent: This vague rib line bounds the right side of the main group of slabby rocks. Other identifying landmarks are the shallow gully immediately to its right and the culminating tower. Otherwise good fortune and the photo-diagram are your best aids to finding the start.

The lower part of the right-bounding gully is not so well defined. Ascend a shallow rib right of the true watercourse then, where the gully becomes more distinct, gain the ridge to its left. Interest increases as the ridge narrows and leads to a gap behind a squat 2m pinnacle at the foot of the Tower.

Start up the little corner behind the pinnacle then swing left after a couple of metres where it becomes difficult. Cross above the corner and trend right to gain the edge overlooking the gully. Trend back left and up a tricky steep section before moving back right to regain the edge. Now carefully ascend blocks on the exposed right edge and continue up the spiky remains of the rib, passing a 5m flake on its left, to gain the plateau above the cwm headwall. Turn right to find the path leading to the summit.

Descent by this route: Not recommended.

Usual descents: As for Route 38. It is also possible to descend back into upper Cwm Cneifion via the stony ribs and runnels at its head.

Combinations: As for Route 36. When approaching via Seniors' Ridge, continue to its second large shoulder before contouring left so as to arrive direct in the upper cwm.

38: SENIORS' RIDGE * (1)

Seniors' Ridge, the blunt north ridge of Glyder Fawr, separates the high and remote hanging valley of Cwm Cneifion from the deeper and much larger hollow of Cwm Idwal. Its Cneifion flank is short and unremarkable whereas the Idwal flank, a succession of rock slabs 400m high, is one of the most dramatic sights in Snowdonia. Unfortunately the ridge crest itself is broad and comparatively uninteresting. Redeeming features are relative neglect, unusual views, and the possibility of spicing up the ascent by one of several exciting approaches up the Idwal face.

Summary: A devious approach to a broad and uneventful ridge.

Conditions: A suitable ascent for most conditions, though low cloud will complicate route-finding during the approach.

Approach: Via the A5 from Capel Curig or Bethesda. Park at Ogwen Cottage (GR:649 604), or at overspill parking areas to the east. Follow the path into Cwm Idwal. From about halfway along the lakeside path, strike diagonally rightwards up the generally pathless grass hillside to gain the floor of lower Cwm Cneifion. Contour rightwards (west) to gain the ridge at a level shoulder. One hour.

Ascent: Ascend the broad back of the ridge, seeking or avoiding difficulties at will, to the rock-littered summit slopes of Glyder

Fawr.

Descent by this route: When descending Seniors' Ridge, remember that it terminates in the comparatively difficult wall ascended by the Direct Approach and so take care not to descend beyond the contouring line into lower Cwm Cneifion.

Usual descents: Descend north-west via unpleasant scree paths (cairned) to Llyn y Cwn, and then via the Devil's Kitchen Path into Cwm Idwal. Location of the path requires care: from Llyn y Cwn, follow the path north-east to enter a stone-filled runnel and thus down onto a broad ramp which slants diagonally across the face to the entrance of the actual Devil's Kitchen cleft.

Combinations: From the summit of Glyder Fawr, circle the head of Cwm Cneifion and descend via the Gribin Ridge (Route 34).

39: DIRECT APPROACH TO SENIORS' RIDGE * (2)

Counteracts a lack of scrambling interest on the previous route with a contrived approach close under the East Wall of the Idwal Slabs. Alternatively it may be ascended as a prelude to scrambles of otherwise short duration in Cwm Cneifion.

Summary: Approaches a simple ridge scramble via a series of open gully/grooves and short chimneys, culminating in an exposed breach of the retaining wall.

Conditions: Drainage from the East Wall affects the lower grooves after prolonged bad weather. The route is often used by climbers descending from the Idwal Slabs and consequently the rock is highly polished. Although only the section which breaches the East Wall is exposed, a slip from any of the lower grooves would also have serious consequences.

Approach: As for Route 38 to the lakeside path in Cwm Idwal. Continue to the foot of the Idwal Slabs, the huge expanse of gently angled rock which faces west beyond the lake (GR:644 589). Thirty minutes.

Ascent: The left side of the Idwal Slabs curls over to form the retaining East Wall. In general the route ascends cracks and shallow grooves in the vegetated, slabby rock overshadowed by this wall.

A 20m-high rectangular slab lies recessed to the left of the main sweep of slabs. Ascend a cracked minor slab to its left then trend left up a polished ramp. Continue more easily to a grassy bay then ascend a gully/groove between quartz slabs on the right and a vegetated area on the left.

The line now continues close under the East Wall and includes a short, awkward chimney. Above a minor final obstacle - a shallow and reclining wide crack close under the fearsome Suicide Wall - take the path trending left to enter a couloir. To the right you will now see a vegetated break leading to a grass ledge and saplings (if they survive) with smooth walls above and below: THIS IS A FALSE LINE. Instead, continue up the rock bed of the couloir for 20m or so and hence locate the correct breach line - a series of highly polished footholds which rises rightwards above the smooth walls. The scrambling here is exposed but no more difficult than anything encountered below.

Above the breach, follow the two polished grooves leading rightwards to a platform (cairn) at the base of Seniors' Ridge. Ascend via short walls and grass terraces (easiest line usually found on the left) to a junction with the normal route at the level shoulder after its Cwm Cneifion approach. Continue to the summit of Glyder Fawr as for Route 38.

Descent by this route: Not recommended without prior knowledge. It is absolutely vital to locate the cairned platform above the two grooves before attempting to find the breach in the East Wall. The breach itself can be unnerving in descent, and the lower gully/grooves disproportionately awkward.

Usual descents: As for Route 38.

Combinations: This is a useful approach to Cwm Cneifion's more difficult scrambles (Routes 36 and 37). Simply quit the route at the level shoulder and contour left into the cwm.

40: IDWAL STAIRCASE AND CONTINUATION ** (2)
The north-west face of Glyder Fawr rises from lakeside to summit in a discontinuous series of slabs and reclining buttresses. This route exploits an uncharacteristic fault line in the lower section to

gain rough slabs above the rock climbing territory on the lower left side of the face. Thus it gains Seniors' Ridge with more style and only slightly more difficulty than either of its two neighbours.

The hideous Staircase section will delight gully freaks. A worrying initial 8m on usually greasy rock provides the most difficult scrambling on the route - a useful early warning.

Summary: A gloomy start up a water-washed fault contrasts with open scrambling on slabby rock above. Simple ridge scrambling to finish.

Conditions: A stream sluices down Idwal Staircase in all but the driest weeks of the year. Spray feeds lichen on the surrounding rocks and so, paradoxically, the most water-worn areas prove to be the least slippery. Nevertheless, it is worth choosing a dry day if only to get the best from the upper slabs (which catch the afternoon sun). Few people ascend the Staircase or explore its continuation rocks, preferring instead the crowded familiarity of the Idwal Slabs.

Approach: As for Route 38 to the lakeside path in Cwm Idwal. Continue to the foot of the Idwal Slabs, the huge expanse of gently angled rock which faces west beyond the lake (GR:644 589). Thirty minutes.

Ascent: An overhung gully, black and water-washed, defines the far right-hand side of the Idwal Slabs.

Ascend for 8m on narrow ledges, worryingly greasy and unhelpfully flat, to where the Staircase darkens beneath the curling roof. Thankfully the angle eases a little here, and rock spikes begin to appear. Continue in this comforting manner until within a couple of metres of large, jammed boulders where the slit curves left towards the waterfall. Traverse narrow ledges leftwards to drier, spiky rock beyond the watercourse and ascend to easier ground.

Continue scrambling in a line 10-20m left of the watercourse, over a rock barrier, until level with the uppermost waterfall. Now trend left towards orange-tinted slabs of rough rock and ascend these at will on good holds (roped parties will find belays at regular intervals though few intermediate runners). Continue more or less directly to emerge on Seniors' Ridge a short distance below the point of arrival of Route 38 from Cwm Cneifion.

Descent by this route: Difficult to locate and even more difficult to execute. Not recommended.

Usual descents: As for Route 38.

Combinations: As for Route 39.

41: NORTH-WEST FACE ROUTE * (2)

Provides an approach to Seniors' Ridge which is more open, though less satisfying, than either of the two previous routes. It takes the buttress right of the Idwal Staircase then finds a way up rocky slopes in the centre of the face before joining Seniors' Ridge below its final rise.

The rock is excellent throughout and, despite lack of traffic, heather does not intrude. Requires some astute route-finding in the upper part to avoid excessive difficulties.

Summary: Open, slabby scrambling on an introductory buttress to grass terraces in the centre of a large face. More good scrambling on a supporting buttress to rock shelves leading deviously onto a broad-backed ridge. Easy scrambling up the ridge to the summit.

Conditions: Does not suffer the drainage which affects the previous two routes and so dries quickly on breezy summer days. Catches the afternoon sun.

Approach: As for Route 38 to the lakeside path in Cwm Idwal. Continue to the foot of the Idwal Slabs, the huge expanse of gently angled rock which faces west beyond the lake (GR:644 589). Thirty minutes.

Ascent: Continue on the path to where, at a stream, it touches the lowest rocks of the right-bounding buttress of the main sweep of the Idwal Slabs (the wet, black and overhung gully of Idwal Staircase, the start of Route 39, bounds the left side of this buttress).

A blunt rib and grass furrow on the buttress front are bounded on the right by blank slabs. Ascend the furrow and then the vague rib between furrow and slabs, curving right, to where the line is broken by a gully coming up from below. Scramble straight up to gain the top of this introductory buttress.

Bryant's Gully, Glyder Fawr

To the right a rock spur protrudes from grass slopes: climb or by-pass the spur to gain the grass couloir which descends from a notch in Seniors' Ridge. Pleasant scrambling on the large, satisfying holds of a buttress right of the couloir leads to a 15m smooth section which guards an obvious horizontal quartz band. Trend right below the smooth section to gain the band at a large and sloping quartz-covered ledge.

A terrace system now leads intricately leftwards, eventually gaining the broad back of Seniors' Ridge which can be followed without further difficulty to the summit.

Descent by this route: Impractical and unappealing.

Usual descents: As for Route 38.

Combinations: As for Route 39.

42: BRYANT'S GULLY ** (2)

Esgair Felen, the south-west spur of Glyder Fawr, presents itself to the lower Llanberis Pass as a huge triangular face of outcrop-studded scree slopes. Those outcrops closest to the road are frequented by rock climbers, though few venture onto the tottering cliffs above. Bryant's Gully follows a shallow gully line which extends from the valley floor almost to the crest of the Esgair. It is probably the only worthwhile scramble on the south side of the Glyders.

Excellent line and impressive rock scenery outweigh a limited outlook and occasionally dismal atmosphere. Some obstacles are difficult when taken direct - especially in poor conditions - though for the most part they are not too serious.

Summary: A gully line ascended in three distinct stages - water-worn steps, an open trough, and a defined upper section between rock walls. Short obstacles occur throughout its length.

Conditions: As in most gullies, expect to encounter some poor rock. However, scree and drainage are less troublesome than might be expected.

Hard start to Main Gully Ridge (Route 30), Glyder Fach

Approach: Leave the Llanberis Pass road at GR:625 568 (several lay-bys for parking nearby) and ascend grass and scree near the stream course. The stream issues from a gully, tree-filled at its base, which splits an area of broken crags to the right of Carreg Wastad, a 60m-high rectangular crag situated a few hundred metres up the hillside. Ten minutes.

Ascent: Narrow and well defined from the outset, the gully leads to the trees with occasional easy steps. Now surmount a smooth boulder to gain a small bay, beyond which a variety of chockstones and a final difficult step lead onto the open hillside at the end of the first section.

The gully opens out as a trough in heather slopes but soon narrows between walls. Cunningly climb a step with a jammed boulder to enter an alcove. The trap is now sprung. The back right wall - unpleasant though not quite so difficult as it first seems - is the best escape (a rope would offer little security on this serious pitch; if in doubt exit up slopes on the right just below the step with the jammed boulder, returning to the gully above the alcove). A second recess with a back wall of curious black rock is also taken on the right.

The gully now begins to curve rightwards (an enticing variant rising leftwards from here involves difficult scrambling on loose rock). Once gained, the groove to the right of a dividing riblet in the gully offers pleasant scrambling until the whole gully line loses identity in a bowl of red scree.

It remains only to pick a way up short walls to emerge at a spectacular viewpoint. Continue up the crest of Esgair Felen to the summit of Glyder Fawr.

Descent by this route: A descent is feasible but not recommended without prior knowledge gained during an ascent.

Usual descents: Descend steeply north-west by a cairned scree path to Llyn y Cwn then cross boggy ground westwards to find the well-defined path which descends to Gwastadnant, about 1.5km farther down the Llanberis Pass from the starting point.

The direct route on East Gully Ridge (Route 31), Glyder Fach

Combinations: Either the Gribin Ridge (Route 34) or Seniors' Ridge via the Cwm Cneifion approach (Route 38) would make an appropriate easy scramble for those wishing to descend into the Ogwen Valley.

Y GARN (947m)

Y Garn is the highest of several summits on the northern limb of the dog-leg Glyders ridge. When viewed from Llyn Ogwen its shape has been likened to that of an armchair, with the abrupt North-East Ridge (normal ascent and descent route) on the right, pinnacled East Ridge (Route 44) on the left, and tiny Llyn Clyd nestling on the seat between. Note that these ridges have been re-named in this edition of the guide to avoid confusion. The south-east flank, which is also used as a normal route of ascent and descent, slopes gently down to Llyn y Cwn in its marshy saddle. The north-east side of this saddle drops sharply into Cwm Idwal as the Devil's Kitchen Cliffs up which Route 43 finds a way.

Before going any further we need to sort out some terminology. In this book the *Devil's Kitchen Cliffs* refers to the entire group of buttresses, otherwise known as Clogwyn y Geifr, which stands at the head of Cwm Idwal. The *Devil's Kitchen* is the central deep rift in these cliffs out of which there is no easy exit. The *Devil's Kitchen Path* is the normal ascent/descent route on the ramp which slants up leftwards from the Devil's Kitchen entrance towards Llyn y Cwn.

43: DEVIL'S KITCHEN AND THE SHEEP WALK * (2/3 or 1)

Though this route is merely an alternative approach to the south-east flank ascent route, it does provide an opportunity to explore the dripping interior of the Devil's Kitchen.

The normal path to Llyn y Cwn ascends a widening terrace to the left of the Devil's Kitchen; the narrower and more exposed Sheep Walk is its near mirror image on the cliffs to the right. There is not much scrambling on the Sheep Walk itself, and even that is not particularly enjoyable, which explains the detour into the Devil's

Kitchen.

Summary: An exploratory detour into a dark, stream-flushed cleft followed by easy scrambling up a scenic terrace.

Conditions: The Devil's Kitchen is always wet but it's worth allowing the stream to subside after heavy rain.

Approach: From Capel Curig or Bethesda along the A5 to a car park at Ogwen Cottage (GR:649 604), or use overspill parking in lay-bys farther east. Take the path behind the toilet block, fork right after a few metres, then ascend through a quarried rift, exiting on the right at its end. Cross a ladder stile and follow a less obvious path, over a second stile, to a mound overlooking Llyn Idwal. Take the path on the west shore of the lake and ascend among boulders to the Devil's Kitchen entrance - the central dark cleft in cliffs at the head of the cwm. Forty-five minutes.

Ascent: a) *Devil's Kitchen:* Scramble up the stream bed over assorted slippery obstacles to the first main test-piece: the huge boulder of the Waterfall Pitch (in dryish conditions the waterfall gushes down behind the boulder). You have four alternatives from which to choose: an immediate retreat; a 3m struggle up the left side of the boulder; an exit up the gap more or less occupied by the waterfall; and a 6m climb up the right-hand corner.

More wet scrambling over short rises leads past a blade of rock to where the stream plunges 20m into a basin at the back of the cleft. Scary. Needless to say this is as far as we can go without resorting to rock climbing. The descent is best made in exact reverse, possibly with an abseil at the waterfall pitch.

b) *The Sheep Walk:* From the entrance to the Devil's Kitchen, the Sheep Walk terrace curves out rightwards - narrow at first but path-marked - between the main cliff face and a shorter supporting wall. Most of it is walking, with a few bits of scrambling on ribs among scree shortly before the ramp emerges on the south-east slope with a path nearby leading to the summit of Y Garn.

Descent by this route: A descent of the Sheep Walk is a reasonable prospect provided it can be located from above. The reddish scree at its top is a good indicator. Note that there is no descent into the

Devil's Kitchen and Y Garn - approaches and descents

100

Devil's Kitchen itself.

Usual descents: (i) Via the Devil's Kitchen Path. From the emergence of the Sheep Walk or the summit of Y Garn, descend gentle slopes south-east to Llyn y Cwn. Location of the Devil's Kitchen Path requires care: from Llyn y Cwn, follow a path north-east to enter a stone-filled runnel and hence gain a broad ramp which slants diagonally across the face to the entrance of the actual Devil's Kitchen cleft.

(ii) Via the North-East Ridge. Don't confuse this with the East Ridge scramble. From the summit of Y Garn, descend the blunt ridge north for a few hundred metres then fork right to descend the narrow and steeply angled North-East Ridge. Zig-zag down the lower shoulder to the mound on the south shore of Llyn Idwal.

44: EAST RIDGE ** (2)

A low-profile rib on the left side of the stream which issues from Llyn Clyd provides a convenient and straightforward approach to the East Ridge proper. The scrambling on the guarding step and beyond is exposed and satisfying.

Summary: A heathery introductory rib followed by a narrow rock arête.

Conditions: There is some loose rock but this is mostly confined to the easier sections. Not especially popular, and surprisingly so.

Approach: As for Route 43 to the mound overlooking Llyn Idwal. Twenty minutes.

Ascent: Scramble easily up an introductory rib, left of the stream which descends from Cwm Clyd, until it loses identity. Trend left to the base of a triangular buttress which guards the East Ridge.

Avoid a difficult direct ascent of the buttress by scrambling up on the left, returning to the crest as soon as possible. Thereafter take the ridge direct - loose and exposed in places - until it narrows and levels out below a final rise.

Short cracks and a corner on the right lead with better rock to some huge fallen blocks. Continue direct or move left over the blocks and ascend the left edge to easy slopes. Walk around the rim of Cwm Clyd to the summit.

Descent by this route: A feasible descent, with a slight increase in difficulty.

Usual descents: As for Route 43.

FOEL GOCH (831m)

Foel Goch is rarely climbed in its own right - this being the unfashionable end of the Glyders - but more often in combination with a walk over Y Garn or Carnedd y Filiast. When viewed from Llyn Ogwen the formidable skyline ridge of Yr Esgair dramatises an otherwise unremarkable mountain.

Cwm Coch bites deep into the eastern side of the mountain. It is bounded on the left by a broad-backed shoulder supported by the bristling crags of Creigiau Gleision, and on the right by Yr Esgair, the north-east ridge.

Two routes are described: a ridge on Creigiau Gleision, and Yr Esgair itself.

45: NEEDLE'S EYE ARÊTE * (3)

The left-hand side of Creigiau Gleision crumples into a series of saw-toothed arêtes interspersed with scree chutes. The Needle's Eye Arête is merely one among many, and its purity of line is apparent only in retrospect.

The route has a distinctly alpine flavour, with continuous and often exposed scrambling on which rope protection may be desirable.

Summary: Difficult scrambling up a pinnacled arête on an unfrequented crag.

Conditions: Although the rock is intrinsically sound, some of the blocks are precariously balanced and demand care. The cliff is rarely visited and so the rock is covered in lichen; this does not interfere with the ascent unless wet, in which case the route is best avoided.

Approach: From Capel Curig or Bethesda along the A5. At either

Ty'n-y-maes or Ogwen Cottage, take the old road onto the west side of the Nant Ffrancon valley. Limited parking. (i) From between the farms of Pentre (GR:639 615) and Blaen-y-nant (GR:642 608), strike directly up the hillside into Cwm Coch. Thirty minutes. (ii) From the bridge just before the road drops steeply down to Blaen-y-nant, take a rising traverse right (faint path) to join a main path above a rock bluff. Follow this rightwards, with a short descent below an outcrop, to a scree slope. Ascend diagonally right up a grass couloir and continue in the same line with some easy scrambling to emerge in Cwm Coch a short distance below the cliff. Forty minutes.

Ascent: A shallow scree runnel bounds the cliff on the left and gouges the grass hillside below. To its right a stone wall, which originates from a sheep fold on a knoll to the left, runs up to an outcrop at the base of the cliff. Right again a scree couloir issues from a gully - Eastern Gully - that winds up into the heart of the cliff. Needle's Eye Arête bounds the gully on its right.

Take the easy lower part of the gully to a rock barrier which is often wet (grass cols appear on the right and left skylines here). From the col on the right, follow a ledge leading back left above the step. More easy scrambling leads to where the gully has become scree-filled (the gully can be followed throughout by easy but loose scrambling at grade 1/2).

Traverse right to gain the arête below an uncompromising step. Creep rightwards beneath a bulge and go up a heather runnel to regain the arête at a notch overlooking Eastern Gully. Ascend a slab on the edge, and the subsequent exposed arête, to a hole in the rock - the Needle's Eye. Now either surmount the step above direct on perched blocks of doubtful stability, or dodge it on the left by an awkward heather traverse, regaining the arête via a short wall.

Continue more easily up the exposed arête to another step, which is taken direct to pinnacles. It is possible to escape left into the gully from here, but the worst is already over. Beyond several more short rises, all of which can be taken direct, the arête emerges onto the east shoulder a little to the right of Eastern Gully.

Foel Goch ridges and approaches

Ascend the shoulder over a slight col onto grass slopes leading north to the summit.

Descent by this route: Not recommended.

Usual descents: From the summit descend south then curve east, crossing a slight col, onto the east shoulder above Creigiau Gleision. Descend the steepening shoulder then veer right to the bank of the stream draining Cwm Cywion. Follow the stream with occasional rightward deviations (stiles) to gain the old road near the bridge at the start of approach (ii).

Combinations: Walk south to the summit of Y Garn and descend by the East Ridge (Route 44).

46: YR ESGAIR (3)

This thoroughly nasty scramble has been included only for completeness. The route follows the north-east ridge, obvious and direct. A prominent notch separates the low-angled lower ridge from its steeply-angled continuation. Absence of belay anchors and difficult scrambling ensure that escape from the notch is a hazardous affair. Technical difficulties ease thereafter, yet the terrain remains treacherous and a lack of easy escape is the strongest motive for continuing. Only those experienced in dangerous terrain should consider an ascent, and they would be wise not to bother.

Summary: A tedious approach to a blunt ridge ascended with loose and unpleasant scrambling above a dangerous start.

Conditions: Takes some drainage so wait for a period of dry weather.

Approach: As for Route 45 into Cwm Coch. Forty minutes.

Ascent: Interesting, easy scrambling along the sharp edge of the lower ridge leads to a pronounced notch below the main ridge. The difficulties that lie ahead are now bleakly obvious. This is a good place for second thoughts.

Above the notch a knife-edged arête leads to a heather shoulder at 10m. The hardest moves are at the top, not helped by the appalling prospect of a fall into the gulch on the right. There are no belay anchors on the shoulder. If repulsed, and you are still determined, the arête can be avoided by descending into the gully on the right to climb a wet, shattered wall using dubious holds and collapsing ledges.

Beyond the heather shoulder the ridge rears up in a continuous line to the summit: ascend it, technically straightforward but insecure, making the best use of shattered leaves on the left and vegetated furrows on the right. The ridge ends abruptly a few metres from the summit and thus almost redeems itself.

Descent by this route: Forget it.

Usual descents: As for Route 45.

Combinations: As for Route 45.

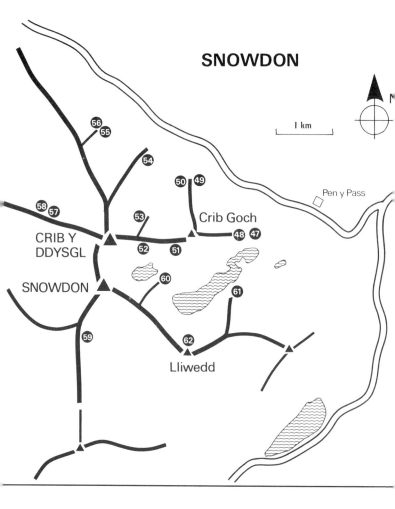

SNOWDON

I km

Pen y Pass

Crib Goch

CRIB Y
DDYSGL

SNOWDON

Lliwedd

Snowdon Group

Snowdon and its satellites form the southernmost of the three highest mountain groups in North Wales, combining the scale of the Carneddau with the ruggedness of the Glyders. The impressions are of open valleys and bulky summits, yet also of rocky cwms and knife-edged ridges.

Normal walking routes to Snowdon Summit continue to inspire with grand scenery, despite heavy traffic and clinically reconstructed paths. Reclusive walkers will find more subtle pleasures on the unworn paths of neglected lower hills. For rock climbers the scope is enormous, with a choice ranging from pseudo-alpinism on Lliwedd to technical intricacy on Dinas Mot. The potential for the scrambler is equally diverse, if not as extensive.

The group is contained by the triangle of roads linking Beddgelert, Caernarfon and Pen y Gwryd. Concentrated at the eastern end are the most important peaks - Snowdon, Crib y Ddysgl, Lliwedd and Crib Goch. Close neighbours Snowdon and Crib y Ddysgl dominate the group. Six major ridges radiate from their summits, delineating the corresponding six cwms; the accompanying sketch map reveals their arrangement.

The Llanberis Pass and, to a lesser extent, Nant Gwynant are the best bases. Both have campsites and bunkhouse accommodation. There is also an excellent forestry campsite about 1.5km from Beddgelert on the Caernarfon road. Bed and breakfast and hotel accommodation will be found in and around Llanberis and Beddgelert. There are youth hostels at Bryn Gwynant, Llanberis and Pen y Pass.

Regular bus routes from Caernarfon extend only as far as Nant Peris and Beddgelert. However, in summer the Sherpa bus service completes the circuit around the mountain by linking Beddgelert and Nant Peris via Pen y Gwryd. This service is extremely useful, even to car owners, because it facilitates unusual combinations of ascent and descent routes.

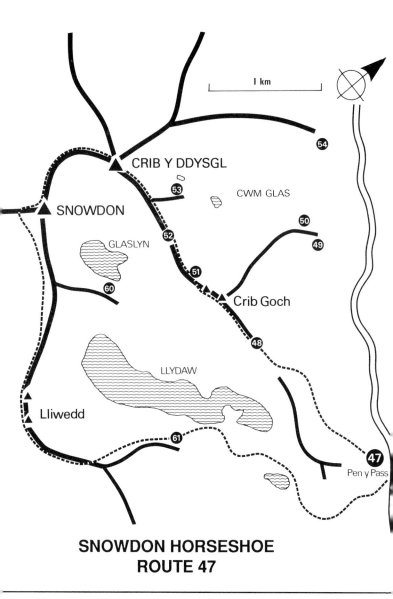

**SNOWDON HORSESHOE
ROUTE 47**

47: THE SNOWDON HORSESHOE *** (1)

This is one of the finest ridge traverses south of Scotland and compares in both quality and difficulty with the Cwm Bochlwyd Horseshoe (Route 10). Given the length of the undertaking, rope protection is impractical - though a short length carried in the rucksack for emergencies is a wise precaution. Three sections require special care: the initial rock barrier and scoop on the East Ridge; the traverse of the Pinnacles on Crib Goch itself; and the first step on Crib y Ddysgl.

If conditions deteriorate badly while on Crib Goch then an emergency descent can be made north-west from Bwlch Coch towards Llyn Glas, or south towards Glaslyn. In either case take care in mist to avoid outcrops and steep scree. If bad weather or darkness approaches while on Snowdon then consider descending via the Pig Track or Miners' Track rather than being forced to abandon the route at Bwlch y Saethau with no easy descent to Pen y Pass.

For convenience the route is described in full here, although its constituent parts, worthy scrambles in their own right, are also described separately: East Ridge of Crib Goch (Route 48); traverse of Crib Goch (Route 51); Crib y Ddysgl (Route 52); traverse of Lliwedd (Route 61).

Summary: A classic ridge traverse, including a horizontal knife-edged section, of about six hours duration.

Conditions: The rock is not totally reliable and must be handled with discrimination. Avoid wet or blustery weather, conditions which make the crossing of Crib Goch nerve-wracking and treacherous.

Approach: From Llanberis or Capel Curig along the A4086 to a car park (fee) at Pen y Pass (GR:647 556). When full, as is frequently the case during weekends and holiday periods, park opposite the Pen y Gwryd Hotel (GR:661 558) and walk up to Pen y Pass in twenty minutes.

Ascent/Descent:
(i) *East Ridge of Crib Goch:* From the upper car park follow a well-marked path westwards to the prominent col of Bwlch y Moch.

111

Beginning the traverse of Crib Goch on the Snowdon Horseshoe (Route 47)

Turn right and approach the blunt East Ridge. The first difficulties arise above a cairned shoulder. An obvious solution is to take a well-scratched, right-slanting line across fluted rock. A cunning alternative slants up left before returning to the right (above the steep part) along an exposed ledge. Seventy metres of sustained scrambling up a shallow depression above the barrier completes the difficult lower part of the ridge.

Flanking paths tempt you left or right away from the shattered rock steps which characterise the upper part of the ridge. Nevertheless it is best to stay on the crest, where the rock is firmest.

The East and North ridges converge at the east end of Crib Goch (literally 'Red Comb'). Although this is not the highest point on the ridge, nor even a prominent top, it is generally referred to as Crib Goch summit.

(ii) *Traverse of Crib Goch:* The first section, across a rock table, is simple enough, then the ridge narrows to a ragged knife-edge. Some walk along this section no-hands, while others find footholds on the left side and use the crest like a handrail.

Eventually the ridge eases and dips to the base of the first of the three Pinnacles. Flank the first on the left, easily, then traverse the left side of the second by a ledge and short scramble to a draughty notch. Now follow a series of exposed ledges slanting from left to right across the right side of the third pinnacle and so gain its summit. Descend a simple gully and scree path to Bwlch Coch.

(iii) *Crib y Ddysgl:* The ridge traverse resumes under the name Crib y Ddysgl; easy at first, then more testing where the rocks coalesce at the far side of an uncharacteristic plateau. Ignore the temptation of a flanking path on the left and tackle the initial obstacle direct. Surmount the succeeding barrier by a series of zig-zags up little chimneys and over blocks on the left side (always within ten or fifteen metres of the crest). The ridge reclines above into a shattered crest of short problems separated by longer stretches of walking. A trig point identifies the summit.

(iv) *Traverse of Snowdon:* Circle the rim of the Glaslyn cwm, passing the 3m marker stone at the exit of the Pig Track Zig-zags, to the summit of Snowdon.

Resist an unpleasant direct descent to Bwlch y Saethau and instead go down the south-west ridge for about 200m to a 2m-high marker stone. Leave the ridge here and descend a scree path (the upper section of the Watkin Path) diagonally across the south face to Bwlch y Saethau. Continue along the path (or ridge to its left) to a large cairn at Bwlch Cilau below the north-west ridge of Lliwedd.

(v) *Traverse of Lliwedd:* The ascent to Lliwedd, which looked so daunting from Snowdon, unfolds without complication. Stay near the left edge for the best scrambling and for tremendous views across the huge north-east face.

Circle over the two summits and a minor top then fork left and scramble down ledges onto scree. Continue by an improving path to the shore of Llyn Llydaw and a junction with the Miners' Track. Follow the track to Pen y Pass.

CRIB GOCH (923m)

Crib Goch is the closest of the four Horseshoe peaks to Pen y Pass, from where it appears as a ruddy pyramid rising above the green hummocks of the neglected first nails. From here the East Ridge appears on the left and the North Ridge on the right, whereas the knife-edged and pinnacled Crib Goch (literally the 'Red Comb') itself is hidden on the far side. The flanks of the mountain are largely composed of an unappealing mixture of rock and scree; only the three ridges and their supporting buttresses are at all sound. There are no easy walking routes to the summit.

Usually an ascent is made by the East Ridge, followed by a traverse of Crib Goch and finishing with an ascent to Snowdon via Crib y Ddysgl. This is what is meant by 'doing Crib Goch', as opposed to 'doing the Horseshoe' which implies continuing beyond Snowdon by traversing Lliwedd.

For convenience these elements of the Snowdon Horseshoe have been described together as Route 47. Those wishing to vary the route, for instance by an approach via the North Ridge, or a descent from Bwlch Coch, can extract the relevant bits of description from there.

48: EAST RIDGE ** (1)

This is the normal route up Crib Goch and is used as a preliminary to a traverse of Crib Goch on the first leg of the Snowdon Horseshoe. Refer to Route 47 for details.

Summary: Mostly straightforward scrambling up a blunt, narrowing ridge after overcoming a tricky lower barrier.

Conditions: As for Route 47.

Approach: Refer to Route 47.

Ascent: Refer to Route 47.

Descent by this route: Descend in exact reverse of the ascent. Prior knowledge of the route in ascent helps when finding the best line through the lower barrier. Take care in mist not to stray into false lines leading away from the ridge. If in doubt, stay close to the crest.

Usual descents: Via the traverse of Crib Goch (refer to Route 47).

Combinations: Refer to Route 47.

49: NORTH RIDGE * (1)

The truncating cliffs of Dinas Mot bar direct access to the long, gently rising North Ridge of Crib Goch and so help preserve its obscurity. Though not as fine as the popular East Ridge, some may prefer the quieter surroundings.

  Though much of the rock is shattered, the scrambling is not technical and the tricky section is really quite short. Route-finding is simple once established on the ridge crest.

Summary: A ridge walk culminating in an exposed scramble across a knife-edge.

Conditions: Avoid windy weather.

Approach: From Llanberis or Capel Curig along the A4086. (i) Park (fee) at Pen y Pass (GR:647 556) or, when this is full, as is frequently the case during weekends and holiday periods, park opposite the Pen y Gwryd Hotel (GR:661 558) and walk up to Pen y Pass in twenty minutes. Follow the Pig Track for about 1km then bear right on a long traversing path, cairned but vague and frequently boggy, to a shoulder on the North Ridge above the cliffs of Dinas Mot. One hour. (ii) Park near Pont y Gromlech (GR:629 566), cross a stile near the bridge and take the path - becoming bouldery - almost to the foot of the central trapezoid slab of Dinas Mot. Ascend diagonally left up tiring scree to avoid the cliffs and enter a boulder-filled canyon. Now traverse rightwards, rising steadily with some scrambling and passing above the exit of the gully which defines the left side of the cliffs, to a shoulder on the North Ridge. Forty-five minutes.

Ascent: Above the shoulder the broad ridge rises gently over grass and slabs. Eventually it steepens into a barren, moonscape ridge and finally narrows to a rock rib. Where the angle eases, the rib narrows further into a knife-edged arête. The side walls of the arête are shattered and so the most secure line takes the exposed crest direct. It ends abruptly at a junction with the East Ridge near the summit.

Descent by this route: A viable descent, though without prior knowledge it can be difficult to find the way off from the shoulder above Dinas Mot. Not recommended in poor visibility.

Usual descents: Via the East Ridge (Route 48).

Combinations: Approach via Route 50. Refer to Route 47 for the continuation to Snowdon.

50: NORTH RIDGE VIA JAMMED BOULDER GULLY ** (3)

Where Dinas Mot curves rightwards into Cwm Glas the cliffs break up into a series of buttresses separated by deep gullies. One of these gullies, Jammed Boulder, provides an approach to the North Ridge at the upper limit of scrambling technicality.

Though short the difficulties are considerable. Moreover, there are no easy escapes from the gully and conditions are rarely ideal. In mitigation the route can be adequately protected with a few long slings.

Summary: Difficult scrambling in an enclosed, damp gully to a shoulder on the North Ridge.

Conditions: The rock is generally sound but becomes coated in green slime during poor weather.

Approach: As for Route 49 to below the central, trapezoid slab of Dinas Mot. Cross the ladder stile on the right and contour below cliffs until beneath the first large recess in the barrier. Gullies define the left and right sides of an inset buttress; gain the base of the left-hand gully, which is further identified by the huge jammed boulder at half height. Thirty minutes.

Ascent: Scramble easily up the gully to a steepening and overcome a 3m block by its left side (slabs to the right of the block slope awkwardly and are insecure when damp).

Above is a bottomless cave formed by the huge boulder. Jammed blocks in the roof offer sling protection for moves left onto an undercut slab on which the holds, though good, are difficult to see in the gloom. The consequences of a slip from here are all too obvious. However, the first moves are the most difficult and better holds soon lead - rucksack permitting - through a hole in the roof to a large bay. Alternatively, ascend the outside route on the right side of the boulder to the bay (not recommended in damp conditions). If required, retreat from the bay is best made by abseil down the outside route using a threaded block anchor.

The gully rises in two stages above the bay. The first steps can be taken direct or by difficult, drier climbing up the rib on the right. Continue ovtered rock then step out onto a jammed block (good thread runner), squeeze through the gap and so gain easier scrambling leading to the shoulder on the North Ridge below its rock section.

Ascend to the summit as for Route 49.

Descent by this route: Not recommended without prior knowledge in ascent. Not as difficult as you might expect, though it is tempting to abseil from the bay above the jammed boulder (which defeats the object).

Usual descents: It is possible to quit the route at the shoulder, in which case refer to the Route 49 approaches for the descent. Otherwise descend the East Ridge of Crib Goch (Route 48).

Combinations: Refer to Route 47 for the continuation to Snowdon. It is possible to traverse easily into Cwm Glas from a higher shoulder on the North Ridge and then ascend Crib y Ddysgl via the Clogwyn y Person Arête (Route 53).

51: TRAVERSE OF CRIB GOCH *** (1)

This famous traverse, the highlight of the Snowdon Horseshoe, is fully described in Route 47.

Summary: Straightforward but exposed scrambling along a knife-edged and pinnacled ridge.

Conditions: As for Route 47. Avoid during windy weather.

Approach: Via the East Ridge (Route 48), North Ridge (Route 49), or Jammed Boulder Gully (Route 50).

Ascent: Refer to Route 47.

Descent by this route: Followed in exact reverse of the ascent, and only marginally more difficult.

Usual descents: Refer for Route 47.

Combinations: Refer to Route 47.

CRIB Y DDYSGL (1065m)

Carnedd Ugain, or Crib y Ddysgl as it is widely known (strictly, Crib y Ddysgl refers only to the continuation ridge of Crib Goch), is too often eclipsed by the grander presence of Snowdon to establish itself as a mountain worthy of ascent in its own right. Yet of the two it has much more to offer the scrambler: within the complex north-eastern cirque of Cwm Glas; on the Llechog Buttress which flanks the long northern ridge; and, to a lesser extent, on the magnificent cliff of Clogwyn Du'r Arddu which darkens its north-western slope.

Cwm Glas is one of the wildest and most impressive glaciated cirques in Snowdonia. The cwm rises in two stages to the remote upper bowl amid tremendous rock scenery. On the left here are red screes below the jagged profiles of Crib Goch and Crib y Ddysgl; on the right a rock-sided ridge which rises almost a thousand metres

from valley floor to summit; and ahead the high crags of Clogwyn y Ddysgl, bounded on their left by the renowned Clogwyn y Person Arête. All three ridges provide worthwhile scrambles.

52: CRIB Y DDYSGL ** (1)

This is the natural continuation to the traverse of Crib Goch on the first half of the Snowdon Horseshoe. It is rarely ascended in its own right and so has been described fully in Route 47.

Summary: A few rises of easy scrambling followed by scenic ridge walking.

Conditions: As for Route 47.

Approach: Via the East or North ridges of Crib Goch (Route 48 or 49) followed by the traverse of Crib Goch (Route 51). A direct approach can be made from Upper Cwm Glas (refer to Route 53 approach) by walking up to Bwlch Coch, the prominent col between Crib Goch and Crib y Ddysgl.

Ascent: Refer to Route 47.

Descent by this route: The ridge provides a straightforward descent to Bwlch Coch. From here descend north into Cwm Glas and return to the Llanberis Pass as for the approach to Route 53.

Usual descents: (i) Descend north along the Cwm Glas Ridge then break off right (east) to descend rocky slopes into Upper Cwm Glas, returning to the Llanberis Pass as for the approach to Route 53. (ii) By the Pig Track. From the summit, descend easily south-west to the 3m marker stone at the exit of the Zig-Zags (GR:608 548) then follow the constructed path east to Pen y Pass.

Combinations: Approach via the North Ridge and traverse of Crib Goch (Routes 49 and 51) and descend by the Cwm Glas Ridge (Route 54).

53: CLOGWYN Y PERSON ARÊTE *** (2 or 3)

Broken ground to the right of Clogwyn y Ddysgl seems to offer an escape from Upper Cwm Glas, but when viewed closely is seen to

Clogwyn y Person Arête, Crib y Ddysgl

On Crib y Ddysgl (Route 52), the Crib Goch Pinnacles in the background

consist of an unstable mixture of scree and shattered rock. Attention turns to the left side of the cliff where a rock ridge rises above the compact slab of the Parson's Nose. This is the Clogwyn y Person Arête, one of the finest natural lines in the area.

Though there are no easy escapes from the arête, the main difficulties are concentrated in the lower part. An alternative start up the edge of the Parson's Nose is more difficult but more pleasantly situated than the usual gully start.

Summary: A long walking approach into a remote cirque escaped via awkward scrambling on a rib or gully wall to a broad-backed ridge. Interesting scrambling on the steps of the easing ridge lead to the summit slopes.

Conditions: Rough, sound rock on the difficult section. Takes little drainage. Best enjoyed when dry. The long approach deters many, so it is rare to encounter more than a few other people.

Approach: From the A4086 Llanberis Pass. Parking in several lay-bys. Cross the river and its tributary at Blaen y Nant (GR:623 570) then ascend steep grass slopes into Cwm Glas. Continue by the west bank of the stream and ascend rocky slopes into Upper Cwm Glas. One hour thirty minutes.

Ascent: From the small pool beyond Llyn Glas the arête appears as a broad spur above the slabby buttress of the Parson's Nose. Gain the crest of the arête above the Nose by one of two approaches: (i) The Western Gully of the Nose, mainly using ledges on the right wall. (ii) By the more difficult rib on the right edge of the Nose itself, ascending widely spaced ledges, some of which overlook the Western Gully. From the top of the Nose a short descent leads to the start of the arête proper (Western Gully arrives here). This latter approach is more in keeping with the open situations found on the arête.

Initially the arête is blunt and the line variable. Some steps are difficult when taken direct, though broad ledges add a sense of security. The easiest way, generally less interesting and on poorer rock, takes a more devious line.

Eventually the angle eases and the arête becomes gradually more broken, turning to scree and merging into the summit slopes.

Llechog Buttress and Ridge, northern spur of Crib y Ddysgl
124

Descent by this route: Not especially difficult, though route-finding is more complex and some of the steps appear intimidating from above. It is best to descend the gully entry rather than the rib start.

Usual descents: As for route 52.

Combinations: Return to the Llanberis Pass via the Cwm Glas Ridge (Route 54) or via Crib y Ddysgl (Route 52) and the traverse and North Ridge of Crib Goch (Routes 51 and 49).

54: CWM GLAS RIDGE * (1)

The ridge which bounds Cwm Glas on its west side gives the most direct ascent to the summit of Crib y Ddysgl. Scrambling interest is confined to the prominent step high on the ridge - small compensation for such a laborious approach. Nevertheless, the views across Cwm Glas are tremendous. A better use for the ridge might be in descent as part of an alternative Horseshoe begun over Crib Goch and Crib y Ddysgl.

Summary: Strenuous walking up a broad ridge topped by a short section of scrambling.

Conditions: The ridge is little used so paths are barely worn.

Approach: Initially as for Route 53, to a break in the high stone wall reached after about ten minutes. Trend right up slopes of grass and stones to gain the broad back of the ridge. Twenty minutes.

Ascent: Ascend the ridge crest (mostly walking) to a level grass section. The ridge now rears up as a spur of broken rock. Take this direct to maximise the amount of scrambling. Beyond a pinnacled crest the ridge steepens once more into a final nose, ascended by scrambling up a recess slightly on the right. Walking remains, veering slightly left to gain the summit of Crib y Ddysgl.

Descent by this route: An uncomplicated descent. Most difficulties can be flanked, usually on the west side.

Usual descents: As for Route 52.

Combinations: Descend this route after ascending via the North Ridge and traverse of Crib Goch (Routes 49 and 51) and Crib y Ddysgl (Routes 52).

The difficult groove on Llechog Buttress (Route 55)

55: LLECHOG BUTTRESS ** (2/3)

The squat buttress of Llechog crowns the west-bounding ridge of unfrequented Cwm Glas-bach, and although an ascent finishes unfashionably low down the mountain, the solitude and quality of scrambling more than compensate.

Route-finding on the buttress itself is complicated so make an effort to positively identify the first perched block before embarking on the main face.

Summary: Intricate and difficult scrambling up a blunt-fronted buttress.

Conditions: The rock is sound but lichenous so wait for dry weather.

Approach: Via the A4086 Llanberis Pass road. Park either at Nant Peris (GR:607 583) or the lay-by at GR:620 572 and walk along the road to Gwastadnant in less than 1km. Cross a bridge over the river and follow the track past buildings at GR:613 575. Ascend the easy-angled, low-profile rib which rises directly to a perched block at the foot of Llechog Buttress. Thirty minutes.

Ascent: A formidable step rises above the perched block. The left-slanting groove is much too difficult, as is the rock above a detached pinnacle on the right, so scramble easily up a vegetated groove on the left side of the barrier, with one slightly awkward move to pass a chockstone on the left. Continue up grass then rock runnels beyond until it is possible to move rightwards onto a platform identified by a 3m block perched near its edge.

Above is a jumble of steep rocks. Go up a left-slanting break, initially by a smooth groove. Above, pull energetically over a chockstone to blocks below a wall. Escape rightwards over blocks to a fine rock platform.

The wall above the platform is hopeless, and the smooth groove on its right side no better. However, the right-hand rib of the groove allows a step right into a dirtier but more amenable groove. Ascend the groove then, immediately above a steepening at wedged flakes, follow a narrow and exposed ramp diagonally left until above the initial groove.

Ledge traverse low down on the East Ridge of Crib Goch (Route 48)

The next step is shorter, more broken and leads directly to a platform with large and small pinnacles. Ascend the left-slanting shattered break behind the pinnacles to a grass bay then scramble up a short, capped chimney (or go 15m up to the right of the pinnacles and ascend a 5m crack in the slab). Trend right and scramble easily up the remainder of the rock spur.

Follow the railway to a junction with the Llanberis Path. Quit the path where it curves right and ascend the broad ridge of grass and stones directly ahead to the summit of Crib y Ddysgl.

Descent by this route: Not recommended.

Usual descents: It is possible to descend directly and unpleasantly between Llechog Buttress and Llechog Ridge, but a more satisfying return to the Llanberis Pass can be made by descending the Cwm Glas Ridge (Route 54).

Combinations: Contour the slope west of Llechog, crossing the railway, to gain the Llanberis Path and then approach and ascend Clogwyn Du'r Arddu as for Route 57.

56: LLECHOG RIDGE * (1 or 2)
The shallow ridge to the right of Llechog Buttress is comparatively uninspiring but provides a useful face-saving alternative if the buttress route proves too difficult.

Summary: Tatty ridge scrambling spiced by a difficult direct start.

Conditions: The rock is generally good but lichenous. Worth waiting for dry weather.

Approach: As for Route 55 almost to the top of the low-relief rib then contour rightwards to a compact tower of rock which terminates the ridge and up to which runs a dry stone wall. Thirty minutes.

Ascent: The tower front is too difficult, as is the chockstone filled crack a few metres up the left side. Left of this is a square-cut slot: scramble up slabby rocks to its left then diagonally right to its easy upper part. Gain the rib on the right and ascend it more easily to the summit of the tower.

Traverse of Crib Goch, (Route 51)

From a grass notch beyond, ascend the difficult face slightly on the left (or avoid it on the right). The stone wall re-appears. Get onto a rib just to its left and ascend this to a shoulder of fallen blocks.

Ascend the next step slightly on the left by a difficult quartz break, dodging a short terminal wall on the left, to where the ridge reclines.

(Note: All the main difficulties can be avoided by gaining this point via slopes of heather and rock on the left side of the ridge.)

Ascend the easier upper part of the ridge at will, the more difficult and interesting scrambling - including a 10m boot-width crack up a slab - generally being found on the right side. Continue to the summit of Crib y Ddysgl as for Route 55.

Descent by this route: Not recommended.

Usual descents: As for Route 55.

Combinations: As for Route 55.

57: EASTERN TERRACE OF CLOGWYN DU'R ARDDU (1)

The gentle north-western cwm abruptly ends in the dark and menacing form of Clogwyn Du'r Arddu - the finest cliff in Wales. The history of first ascents on 'Cloggy' is a long and fascinating one, beginning with that of the Eastern Terrace in 1798 by the Reverends Bingley and Williams in search of plant specimens. But the cliff is not fertile ground for the rock scrambler, and apart from the two scruffy terraces described here there is nothing else of interest.

Summary: Momentarily interesting scrambling on a widening terrace slanting across a huge cliff.

Conditions: The terrace is commonly used as a descent route by rock climbers, though the cliff is busy only during dry spells in summer. Take care not to dislodge scree from the terrace edge as it may fall onto climbers below.

Approach: From the east side of Llanberis on the A4086, follow the narrow surfaced road opposite the Royal Victoria Hotel to a parking place at the top of the hill after 1km (GR:582 589). Walk up the Llanberis Path towards Snowdon until it rises steeply left about 700m beyond Halfway House. Fork right here on a path which contours high above Llyn Du'r Arddu to the foot of the East Buttress. One hour.

Ascent: Viewed frontally the East Buttress appears in the shape of a right-angled triangle, with the East Gully - a hopelessly loose rock climb - forming the upright and the Eastern Terrace the hypotenuse.

The terrace fails to reach the base of the cliff so begin on the left by scrambling up a rising line of scratched rock steps. A zig-zag path then leads to a junction with the terrace, here partially overhung by a huge buttress known as The Boulder.

Scramble leftwards up a series of wet steps close under overhangs to the wider part of the terrace. Zig-zag easily up the left side then ascend the upper scree runnel to grass slopes.

Descent by this route: Not easy to locate from above without prior knowledge, but otherwise a viable descent. Remember to quit the terrace after descending the wet steps under the overhangs.

Usual descents: Ascend featureless slopes to the east, crossing both the railway and the Llanberis Path, to the summit of Crib y Ddysgl and descend as for Route 52. For a direct return to Llanberis, contour east above the cliff and follow the railway to its junction with the Llanberis Path.

Combinations: Approach via Llechog (Route 55 or 56).

58: WESTERN TERRACE OF CLOGWYN DU'R ARDDU (2/3)
The Western Terrace - more difficult and sustained than its eastern counterpart - rises diagonally rightwards beneath the overlapping slabs of the West Buttress. Since publication of the first edition of the guide, a large rockfall has added a sinister new aspect to the ascent; the route is described for completeness, but is probably best avoided.

Summary: Awkward and insecure scrambling along a dramatically situated hanging terrace.

Conditions: Suffers from drainage during and for several days after bad weather, and is then best avoided. Loose rock littering the easier section adds to the feeling of insecurity.

Approach: As for Route 57 to a path division below the East Buttress. The lower path passes below the lowest rocks of the cliff (Middle

Clogwyn Du'r Arddu terraces, north-west flank of Crib y Ddysgl

58

Rock) to below a tall, dripping recess. The terrace is now obvious, overshadowed by a band of overhangs as it slants up to the right. One hour.

Ascent: Gain the terrace a short distance beyond its start by scrambling up a clean 6m groove on good holds. Unpleasant mossy scrambling leads along the terrace to an insecure passage across shattered red rock to the start of the main section below huge overhangs.

Continue up bare rock runnels - easier than it looks - until barred by a 5m wall of curiously pocketed rock. Fortunately this is covered with large holds and can be protected with a rope. (Resist avoiding the wall by ramps on the outer edge; these are smooth and offer little security.)

Ascend rock slabs then creep through poised rockfall debris, later escaping rightwards to grass. Continue up an easy-angled slab then scramble up grass to a flat shoulder above the cliff.

Descent by this route: Not recommended.

Usual descents: As for Route 57.

Combinations: As for Route 57.

SNOWDON (YR WYDDFA) (1085m)

The name *Snowdon* conjures up images of iron rails, pipelines, eroded paths, cafes and crowds, of a mountain abandoned to the tourist. Yet nothing can detract from the pleasure of clambering up its flank to stand on the highest summit in Wales. And it is still possible, even here on a summer bank holiday, to spend an afternoon scrambling without encountering a single other person.

A glance at the sketch map will reveal the arrangement of ridges and cwms better than any description, but the following will serve to establish nomenclature for later use:

Snowdon Summit (as opposed to Snowdon as a whole, which loosely describes a mountain mass that includes Crib y Ddysgl and its cwms and ridges) takes the form of a squat, three-sided pyramid. Three ridges descend from the summit: north towards Crib y Ddysgl, east towards Lliwedd, and south towards Yr Aran. Three cwms lie between these ridges: the Glaslyn cwm east of the summit, Cwm Clogwyn to the west, and Cwm Tregalan to the south.

One of the described scrambles ascends out of Cwm Tregalan onto the South Ridge, the other escapes the Glaslyn cwm by its bounding ridge to finish up the East Ridge.

59: TREGALAN COULOIR * (2)

The southern approach to Snowdon via the Watkin path initially has a picturesque quality more reminiscent of the Lake District than Snowdonia. However, on entering Cwm Tregalan the pleasant glades are left behind and the rubble slopes of Snowdon dominate the view. Below the summit, and as far as Bwlch Main on the South Ridge, the face consists of a jumbled mass of broken rock. Only beyond the Tregalan Couloir does it coalesce into definite buttresses.

Easier variants have been found since the first edition of the guide and so dire warnings about inescapability and difficulty no longer apply. Nevertheless, it remains a serious outing.

Summary: Surprisingly varied scrambling based on a remote gully / couloir.

Conditions: Scree litters the bed of the couloir and so much of the scrambling lies on the flanking buttresses. Drainage does not badly affect the line, though it is wise to avoid periods during and immediately after wet weather. Catches the morning sun in summer. Rarely ascended.

Approach: From Beddgelert or Pen y Gwryd along the A498 to a car park at Bethania (GR:628 507). From the west bank of the river follow the signed Watkin Path via Cwm y Llan to quarry spoil heaps (GR:613 524). Where the Watkin Path curves up to the right, bear left to contour into Cwm Tregalan, initially by a faint path. The couloir is largely hidden from this angle so locate its entrance before approaching the cliff too closely.

A trapezoid buttress, cut on the right by a slanting break, defines the left side of the cliff. A larger, more broken buttress to the right is bounded on its right side by a depression which emerges at the cliff base as a narrow gully beneath a black cleft - the first objective (further right, beyond a smaller buttress of pink-tinted rock, the face

135

degenerates into slopes of rubble). One hour thirty minutes.

Ascent: Avoid the slimy beginnings of the gully by scrambling up rough slabs on the right. Where they steepen, traverse awkwardly left on loose rock then ascend the gully bed to a recess beneath an evil-looking, capped chimney.

The original route ascends the water-worn runnel slanting up to the left from here, then traverses rightwards after about 30m, crossing a buttress to re-enter the couloir. However, this is both difficult and insecure (Grade 3), so instead ascend almost to the base of the chimney then escape rightwards up a break - scruffy but not too difficult. Ignoring easy ground to the right, ascend the buttress front on superbly rough rock. Continue up the buttress as it narrows and eases but then, where it rears up again in a broad and indistinct mass, descend diagonally left to regain the couloir bed some distance above the evil chimney.

After 15m avoid an ugly 8m step by scrambling up clean rock on the left. Regain the bed then, after 10m, avoid another step on the left. Continue up the couloir, or, better, up the shallow rib just to its left until forced into the bed after 30m. There is less scree now so scramble over a few small rises until the couloir fans out. Go up the left side of what is now a shallow, rocky depression to emerge on the South Ridge.

Walk up the South Ridge to Snowdon Summit.

Descent by this route: Not recommended.

Usual descents: (i) By the Watkin Path. Descend south-west from Snowdon Summit along the South Ridge for about 200m to a 2m marker stone; turn left here to descend a slanting scree path to Bwlch y Saethau. Continue to a large cairn at Bwlch Cilau below the north-west ridge of Lliwedd then turn right and follow the obvious path into Cwm Tregalan. (ii) By the South Ridge. Descend south-west from Snowdon summit, veering left at Bwlch Main onto the South Ridge proper. At Bwlch Cwm Llan, at the foot of the South Ridge, turn left and descend diagonally across the grassy hillside - in the lower stages following the course of a dismantled tramway for a few hundred metres - to the entrance to Cwm y Llan and a junction with the Watkin Path.

60: Y GRIBIN AND THE EAST RIDGE ** (1)

The Miner's Track from Pen y Pass contours above Llyn Teyrn, short-cuts across Llyn Llydaw by a restored causeway, then rises steadily to Llyn Glaslyn below the massive north-east face of Snowdon. This route escapes the cwm by ascending the left-bounding rocky spur of Y Gribin to Bwlch y Saethau before toiling up the East Ridge to Snowdon Summit.

Y Gribin compares in difficulty to the East Ridge of Crib Goch, and is rather more enjoyable. Its relative unpopularity can only be attributed to the fact that it emerges at a col, not at a summit.

Summary: Good scrambling up a broad ridge amid impressive surroundings, followed by a second, more broken ridge leading directly to Snowdon Summit.

Conditions: Takes little drainage but is best enjoyed in dry conditions (the lower slabs in particular are insecure when wet). Firm rock on Y Gribin but some loose material on the East Ridge.

Approach: From Capel Curig or Llanberis along the A4086 to a car park (fee) at Pen y Pass (GR:647 556). When full, as is frequently the case during weekends and holiday periods, park opposite the Pen y Gwryd Hotel (GR:661 558) and walk up to Pen y Pass in twenty minutes.

Follow the Miner's Track to the stream exit of Llyn Glaslyn at GR:619 545. One hour fifteen minutes.

Ascent: Cross boulders at the stream outflow and flank a grassy terminating hump to reach a col below the steep part of the ridge.

Ignore loose flanking routes and ascend slabs slightly right of the crest. Continue roughly in the same line, occasionally detouring to the left, to a cairned promontory above the ridge. Trend right to gain Bwlch y Saethau below the East Ridge of Snowdon.

Scramble easily up the blunt, broken ridge to Snowdon Summit.

Descent by this route: An uncomplicated descent, with marginal increases in scrambling and route-finding difficulties.

Usual descents: Via the Pig Track or Miner's Track. From Snowdon Summit descend north-west for about 600m to the 3m marker stone at the emergence of the Zig-zags. Turn right to descend the

Glaslyn flank of Snowdon

constructed path. For the Pig Track, continue along a gradually descending path east to Pen y Pass. For the Miner's Track, bear right where the Pig Track levels after its descent of the Zig-zags and descend steeply to the shore of Llyn Glaslyn.

Combinations: Use Y Gribin as the first or last leg of a shortened Snowdon Horseshoe in combination with a traverse of Lliwedd or Crib Goch and Crib y Ddysgl (refer to Route 47).

LLIWEDD (898m)

Lliwedd is synonymous with the two massive buttresses set dramatically above Llyn Llydaw on its north-east face. The East Peak can offer the scrambler nothing: all routes involve significant technical difficulties. The slightly higher West Peak is the more broken of the two and its easiest climb just qualifies as a scramble. The traverse of north-east and north-west ridges is usually undertaken as the last leg of the Snowdon Horseshoe, but is mentioned here for completeness as a route in its own right.

61: TRAVERSE OF LLIWEDD ** (1)
This less dramatic wing of the Snowdon Horseshoe provides a worthwhile easy scramble in itself.

Summary: Easy scrambling up and down broad-backed ridges.

Conditions: Viable in most conditions. Wind and rain are less of a problem here than on Crib Goch.

Approach: From Capel Curig or Llanberis along the A4086 to a car park (fee) at Pen y Pass (GR:647 556). When full, as is frequently the case during weekends and holiday periods, park opposite the Pen y Gwryd Hotel (GR:661 558) and walk up to Pen y Pass in twenty minutes.

Follow the Miner's Track to the shore of Llyn Llydaw. Thirty minutes.

Ascent: Turn left and follow a path near the shore, passing the valve house and crossing the stream outflow. Ascend the west flank of the north-east ridge, rising steadily over scree and with some easy scrambling, to its crest. Follow a path on the left side of the crest, over Lliwedd Bach, to the summit of East Peak. Continue along the rocky crest to the slightly higher summit of West Peak. Descend the rock steps and terraces of the north-west ridge - stay close to the crest for the best scrambling - the cairned col of Bwlch Cilau at its foot.

Cross the elongated col to Bwlch y Saethau and either ascend to Snowdon Summit via the East Ridge or descend to Llyn Glaslyn via Y Gribin (refer to Route 60).

Descent by this route: The traverse is slightly easier in reverse.

Usual descents: As for Route 60.

Combinations: Refer to Route 47.

62: WEST PEAK VIA BILBERRY TERRACE *** (3)
This route - the best of the most difficult scrambles in this book - ascends a devious but logical line up the West Peak.

Long and inescapable (it is the easiest route on the face), **it should be attempted only in good conditions by skilful and confident scramblers familiar with the serious situations found on big cliffs.** However, belay anchors and runners can be found to protect the most difficult sections (selection of nuts required). The situations, atmosphere and scale are tremendous.

Summary: Varied and frequently exposed scrambling up a huge buttress.

Conditions: The buttress is rarely in good condition outside the period May to October. Allow a few days to dry after wet weather. Best enjoyed early morning (when the face catches the sun) during dry summer weather. The rock is generally sound but expect to find some loose blocks and spikes.

Approach: As for Route 61 to the stream outflow from Llyn Llydaw. When half-way up the first rise towards the north-east ridge, contour right along a narrow path until below the north-east face.

West Buttress of Lliwedd

Ascend scree to below Central Gully, the shallow depression between the two main buttresses.

From the top of a cone of red scree (just right of the mouth of Central Gully), ascend easily up to the right to a worn ledge below a 20m wall which bars access to the lower left end of the Bilberry Terrace - the heather ramp which slants upwards across the face from left to right. At this point Central Gully is about 30m to the left, while 30m to the right, at the foot of the face, is an obvious quartz-capped block. One hour.

Ascent: Scramble up the wall - sustained but not too difficult - then step awkwardly right to gain the lower left end of the terrace. There is a belay a little higher. Scramble more easily up the terrace and across the narrows of a rock ramp to the foot of a 5m corner (belay anchors above the ledge on the right).

Protected by a threaded chockstone in the crack, ascend the corner with conviction. Belay with nuts at its top or continue easily for 6m or so trending left to a blunt spike. Alternatively, avoid the corner from 6m below by ascending left past a block and up heather ledges for 6m then traversing right.

Ignore the horrible wide crack above and instead step up, traverse right (exposed but not too difficult) and struggle up a short, wide crack. Go up the terrace for 7m or so then, ignoring a grassy cul-de-sac, ascend rocks on the left to below a smooth wall. Now ascend a corner on the right to regain the terrace.

Continue up the terrace and over one short rise (ignoring a gully spanned by a rock splinter) to a pinnacle on the apex of the buttress. This is Pinnacle Corner, the half-way point and the end of the easy route-finding.

Pass through the notch, step across to grass ledges and follow them up to the right for 7m. Now traverse narrow ledges to the right for 7m to a larger grass ledge and spike. Though possible to ascend the depression directly to a 2m spike in 30m (care with loose rock), it is better to continue the traverse for a further 5m to its end then go up and left, past a clutter of spikes, to enter the depression above its most difficult section. Avoid the next step on the left then traverse right onto a grass bay. Finally go diagonally left past a huge spike and so in a further couple of metres to the 2m spike.

The rock above is hopelessly difficult so scramble easily leftwards to regain the ridge above Pinnacle Corner. Twenty-five metres to the left is another ridge. Gain it at a notch by descending into a depression then ascending diagonally. Gain a third ridge 30m to the left via connecting ledges. Now, at last, some sort of upward escape is possible.

From the crest, follow heather ledges leading rightwards into a depression. A little higher, overcome a tricky rock barrier then scramble to the top of the face, deviating left and right to find the easiest way and emerging within four strides of the summit.

Descent by this route: Not recommended.

Usual descents: Refer to Route 61.

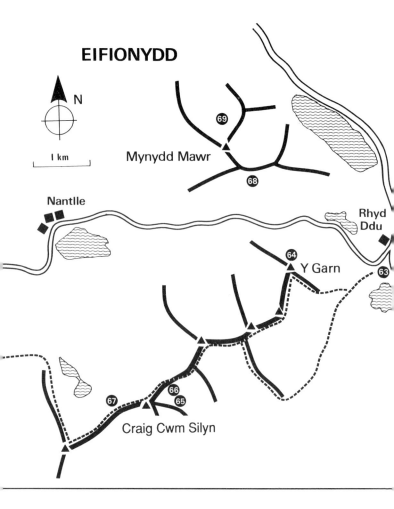

EIFIONYDD

N

I km

Nantlle

Rhyd
Ddu

Mynydd Mawr

Y Garn

Craig Cwm Silyn

Eifionydd

The small hills of Eifionydd exert a feeble pull on mountaineers. No cloud-piercing ridges here, no historically famous rock climbs. Climbers and hillwalkers come here - when they come at all - to relax on the sun-warmed rock of Craig Cwm Silyn or to stroll along the Nantlle Ridge.

There is even less to attract the scrambler. The most likely rock is either choked in vegetation or shattered into treacherous splinters. For this reason all described lines involve difficult scrambling, sometimes on very poor rock. More nervous energy has been expended checking these few routes than twice their number on the Glyders or Snowdon. The exception is the Nantlle Ridge, a simple ridge walk spiced with a few scrambly steps.

The main group of hills - those linked by the Nantlle Ridge - lie to the south of the B4418 between Penygroes and Rhyd Ddu. Mynydd Mawr lies in the angle made by this road and the A4085 from Rhyd Ddu to Caernarfon.

Most people will visit Eifionydd from a base in the main mountain area. Of these, Beddgelert is the most convenient (refer to the introduction to the Snowdon Group). A limited bus service operates between Beddgelert and Caernarfon via Rhyd Ddu, supplemented in the summer months by the Sherpa service.

Access arrangements in Eifionydd are more restrictive and sensitive than elsewhere in the national park. For this reason it is wise to stick to the described approaches.

63: NANTLLE RIDGE *** (1)
A delightful ridge walk on grass enlivened at intervals by sections of simple rock scrambling.

The route is described as a double traverse to prolong interest and solve the logistical problem of arranging return transport.

Summary: By the double traverse, an 18km ridge walk of about seven hours duration which includes isolated sections of simple scrambling.

Approach to Y Garn at the start of the Nantlle Ridge

Conditions: Some sections are vulnerable to cross winds, but otherwise the route is possible in most conditions. Popular during fine summer weekends.

Approach: From Caernarfon or Beddgelert along the A4085 to a large car park on the main road, 0.5km south of Rhyd Ddu village (GR:571 526).

Ascent: Go through a swing gate opposite the car park entrance and follow the signed path to a junction with the Nantlle road (limited parking here).

Turn left immediately and follow the signed path onto the grassy flank of Y Garn. Turn right soon after crossing a ladder stile ("ridge" marked on a rock) and ascend steeply by a narrow path to the summit of Y Garn.

Follow the broad ridge southwards then ascend the narrow, rocky section - staying near the crest for maximum scrambling interest - to the summit of Mynydd Drws y Coed.

Continue along the narrow ridge as it descends then veers right (ignore a contouring path left here). Scruffy, easy scrambling leads to the flat summit of Trum y Ddysgl.

Follow the grass ridge south-west then fork right, descending, to cross a narrowing before rising gradually up its broad continuation to the obelisk at the summit of Mynydd Tal y Mignedd.

Walk south along the grass ridge then descend steeply on an eroded path to the double col of Bwlch Dros Bern. Ascend the rock nose at the far side of the col, scrambling up rocks just right of the crest for most interest (or directly above the stone wall at grade 2). Or avoid all this easily on the right. Continue up the good path beyond to the summit of Craig Cwm Silyn.

Follow a broad and featureless ridge south-west to the final summit of Garnedd Goch.

Descent by this route: Return to Rhyd Ddu by the same route. Scrambling sections are now taken in descent so there is a slight increase in difficulty.

Usual descents: (i) For the single traverse, leave a second vehicle at the road end at GR:496 511 (refer to Route 67 approach). From Garnedd Goch, descend a grass shoulder northwards to a gate in the transverse stone wall. Go through the gate and turn left to follow the track to the road end. (ii) Return along the ridge to the fork a few hundred metres south-west of Trum y Ddysgl summit. Descend south along the crest of an initially steep grass ridge (narrow path) to the boggy col of Bwlch y Ddwy Elor. Cross a stile on the left and follow a good path and track, entering trees, to emerge later at a forestry track. Follow this rightwards for a few metres then bear left on a track leading to a stream. Cross the stream by a bridge on the left and then turn right onto the main track. After a few metres turn left and follow a rough stony path northwards across the base of the eastern slopes of Mynydd Drws y Coed and Y Garn. Enter a boggy area beyond a swing gate but then continue on a good path to rejoin the ascent route at the painted rock.

Combinations: Refer to Routes 64-67 for alternative starts and variants.

Y GARN (633m)

Y Garn, eastern outpost of the Nantlle Ridge, appears wedge-shaped when viewed from Rhyd Ddu. The Nantlle Ridge begins up its grassy south-east flank, while a handful of climbs and a disappointing scramble ascend the rocky north-east face.

64: WESTERN ARÊTE (3)

This mostly unpleasant and insecure route is of little interest except to competent scramblers determined to begin a traverse of the Nantlle Ridge with a tough ascent. A few metres of exposed scrambling high on the arête help to compensate.

Summary: A long approach to a short, precarious scramble.

Conditions: Wait for dry conditions. The face seems to hold moisture for a long time so allow several dry days after prolonged wet weather. Lack of use means that unstable blocks remain.

Approach: Initially as for Route 63. About 100m beyond twin stiles, contour rightwards over grass, scree and then boulders to the stone wall which runs up to the foot of the crags on the north-east face. One hour.

Ascent: Up to the right of the wall is a central heather bay. Eastern Arête is on the left, with Central Gully - grassy and uninteresting - to its right. Right of the central blunt prow of rock is a heather recess below an evil gully, to the right of which - starting at a lower level - is the rock and heather rib of Western Arête.

Gain the lower rib with difficulty from the right side and carefully ascend its crest over loose spikes and blocks to a heather shoulder. All this section can be avoided by scrambling nervously up heather in the high-angle gully/recess on the right.

Ignore easy ground to the right and ascend the upper rib near its left edge for a few blissful moments on exposed and relatively sound rock.

Descent by this route: Not recommended.

Usual descents: Refer to Route 63.

Combinations: Refer to Routes 63, 65 and 66.

CRAIG CWM SILYN (734m)

The highest mountain on the Nantlle Ridge also has the most to offer in terms of rock climbs and scrambles. These are concentrated on the magnificent twin rock prows of uncharacteristically sound rock which overlook Cwm Silyn on the west side of the mountain.

65: PENNANT RIB (3)

A short and difficult scramble useful only as an alternative ascent of the nose above Bwlch Dros Bern when traversing the Nantlle Ridge (Route 63) in a westerly direction.

Summary: Precarious scrambling up a sharp rib.

Conditions: Takes little drainage but must be crisply dry. Faces the morning sun in summer. Take care with suspect blocks on the upper rib. Rarely ascended.

Approach: As for Route 63 to Bwlch Dros Bern (GR:531 507). Contour scree slopes on the south side of the ridge to a recess above and to the right of a stone wall which runs up towards the crags.

Ascent: Within the recess a slender rib rises to the right of an easy scree gully. Ascend the lower part of the rib to the first step, split on its left side by a 5m leg-width crack. Climb the crack, awkward to enter, to a ledge then step right and move up - still difficult - to easier scrambling and a horizontal knife-edge (or avoid these difficulties by entering at this level from the scree gully).

Ascend difficult slabs and a sharp rock edge to start the second step. Continue by a blunt edge - take great care with poised blocks here - until the rib falls back to emerge from the recess near the path leading to the summit of Craig Cwm Silyn.

Descent by this route: Not recommended.

Usual descents: (i) Descend the easy scree gully at the side of the rib to return to the foot of the recess. (ii) Descend the path and scramble down the nose (avoidable by a detour on the north side) to Bwlch Dros Bern.

Combinations: Refer to Route 63.

66: RIGHT-HAND PENNANT RIB (2)

A less difficult alternative to Pennant Rib, lacking its interest but with slightly better rock.

Summary: Heathery scrambling up a blunt rib.

Conditions: Generally as for Route 65, though this rib dries more slowly.

Approach: As for Route 65.

Ascent: Start up the rib right of Pennant Rib by heathery scrambling then complete the ascent of the first rise by a rightward slanting narrow slab.

The rib steepens above. Ascend its right wall then move left when possible to its crest (care with the rock here). Higher, avoid an unstable pile of rocks by moving left then back right on heather - not easy. Finish up a heathery ridge.

Descent by this route: Not recommended.

Usual descents: As for Route 65.

Combinations: Refer to Route 63.

67: CRAIG FAWR RIB ** (3)

Twin rock prows dominate the rocky headwall above Cwm Silyn. That on the right, Craig yr Ogof, is famous for the rock climbs on its slabby west face and vertical front nose. That on the left, Craig Fawr, is larger but more broken and therefore rarely climbed. This route ascends the slender rib on the right-hand side of Craig Fawr and can be used as a preliminary to an easterly traverse of the Nantlle Ridge.

Some experience of easy rock climbs would be an asset, and a rope of at least 36m in length is desirable to reach the best belays. An escape to easy ground can be made from any of the ledges between pitches.

Summary: Three rib pitches of sustained and difficult scrambling on the flanks of a large, secluded buttress.

Conditions: Does not suffer excessive drainage but wait for dry weather. Catches the afternoon sun in summer. The rock is generally good.

Approach: From Nantlle on the B4418 between Rhyd Ddu and Penygroes. Go west from Nantlle and turn left after 2km onto the Llanllyfni road. Turn left again after 1.5km and follow this single-track road for 2km to the end of the surfaced section at GR:496 511 (park in the field just beyond the gate). Continue on foot until the track ends above the Llynnau Cwm Silyn. Contour above the lakes, crossing the hillside to the heather couloir between Craig yr Ogof and Craig Fawr. To the left of the couloir is a heather rib which leads into the first rocks of the rib proper.

Ascent: Ascend the first rib centrally to half height then by its right edge to a heather platform below the 30m main rib pitch.

Start the rib on the right then step left after 6m or so to gain the crest. Climb the crest - sustained but on good rock - to another level area.

Above easy ground are two ribs. Gain these directly or via an entertaining but difficult riblet on the left.

Scramble up the left-hand rib, initially via a staircase, until after 6m the angle falls back and the scrambling eases to a level section. Finally cross a knife-edge to gain the summit plateau.

67

Descent by this route: Not recommended.

Usual descents: (i) Refer to Route 63. (ii) Descend the Great Stone Shoot gully on the west side of the Craig yr Ogof prow to return into Cwm Silyn. This descent can be identified from the edge of the summit plateau by the stone wall and fencing at its top. Where necessary, avoid awkward steps in the gully by descending the rib on its left (looking out), but avoid straying into the couloir even farther left.

Combinations: Refer to Route 63.

MYNYDD MAWR (698m)

This shapely miniature mountain has two faces of interest to the scrambler: the bleached and crumbling south-facing cliffs of Craig y Bera; and the remote and dank north-facing cliffs of Craig Cwm Du. A route has been described on each, though neither escapes the doubtful rock for which these crags are renowned.

68: SENTRIES' RIDGE AND CONTINUATION *** (2 or 3)

Huge buttresses and pinnacled ridges cover almost the entire south flank of Mynydd Mawr, yet few climbers bother (or dare) to come here. Vast screes below the cliffs forewarn of the dangerously friable rock.

Sentries' Ridge takes a well-defined slender line to the right of the large central buttress. The scrambling is prolonged, sustained and varied. An ability to judge rock quality is more important than technical expertise. However, some of the gendarmes are difficult to climb when taken direct. Escape into an easy scree gully is possible at various points.

Summary: Excellent scrambling on suspect rock along a succession of narrow and pinnacled ridges.

Conditions: Faces south and dries quickly on sunny or breezy days. Wait for these good conditions.

Craig Fawr, Craig Cwm Silyn

Approach to Craig y Bera, Mynydd Mawr

Approach: From Caernarfon or Beddgelert along the A4085 to a large car park opposite the Snowdon Ranger Youth Hostel (GR:565 551). Turn right from the car park entrance and walk along the main road towards Rhyd Ddu. Turn right onto a forestry track at farm buildings, just after bridging the lake inflow (no parking here).

Go through twin gates on the track then turn left immediately,

through a gate, and ascend the pasture diagonally rightwards to enter the forest by a gate. Initially follow a good path through trees, then a poorer path along a break line, to emerge from the forest at a ladder stile.

Turn right and ascend near the forest edge. After crossing a stile near the end of the plantation, contour left to scree below the cliffs.

Pass below the first broken buttresses to a large recess from which rises a slender, pinnacled ridge between scree gullies. One hour fifteen minutes.

Ascent: Easy, heathery scrambling on the right side of the ridge leads to the first gendarme. Ascend it directly, including one awkward move, or turn it on the right, returning to the crest after about 6m. Continue up the ridge, passing directly over several pinnacles, to a grass col at the end of the Sentries' Ridge as originally climbed by Archer Thomson in 1910.

Another ridge rises above. Scramble up the edge left of the central heather runnel, if necessary taking difficult sections on the wall overlooking the runnel to minimise the consequences of a slip. Above a heather col, scramble up another shorter ridge to a tunnelled notch.

The ridge above the notch is steeper and more difficult than its predecessors, though the rock is better than appearances suggest. Ascend it directly or avoid it, deviously, via heather and a rock runnel on the right.

Above is a mirror image of the ridge above the grass col; scramble up its right edge to easier ground. Continue up the remainder of the ridge, probably turning the most shattered gendarmes, to heather slopes above the cliff. The path to the summit is nearby.

Descent by this route: Not recommended.

Usual descents: Descend the spur eastwards above the cliffs, rejoining the approach path at the forestry plantation.

69: BEAR BUTTRESS * (2/3)

After a difficult start on the generally good rock of the lower buttress, this intimidating route finishes precariously up a technically easier but unstable final tower. Given that some of the harder sections on the lower buttress can be avoided only by devious and unpleasant means, some may prefer to use a rope and climb them direct. Rope protection would reassure on the final tower also, though one doubts if draping slings over those rickety spikes would ultimately do any good. However, it can be avoided altogether.

Summary: A series of connecting ribs culminating in an exposed and precarious finish.

Conditions: The lichenous rock is slippery in poor weather. Conversely, friction is excellent in dry conditions. North-facing, so allow several dry days after prolonged rain.

Approach: From the A4085 Caernarfon to Beddgelert road. Park at a lay-by at GR:547 563 and cross the track over the bridge 20m towards Caernarfon. After a few minutes turn right on a signed footpath and follow it uphill, entering the forest at a gate. Continue up through the forest until the path dips (view of the crag to the left from here). Go over a stile and cross a meadow between two plantations. Beyond a ladder stile, turn sharp left and follow the wall to a stream. Follow the stream bank into Cwm Du. A transverse heather mound near the head of the cwm provides a good view of the crescent-shaped cliffs of the headwall.

The grass terrace which slants up from left to right on the back wall is Central Rake. It starts a short distance above the base of a deep, dripping gully (Saxifrage Gully) and finishes at a broken arête high on the right-hand side of the buttress. To the left of Saxifrage is Eden Gully, while to the left again is a clutter of lesser ridges, gullies and buttresses. The only easily recognisable landmark in this area is the Crazy Pinnacle, a tottering 10m pedestal near the top of the crag. Left of Crazy Pinnacle is a large, blunt buttress set above ribs and gullies. This is Bear Tower, the final obstacle of the vague but logical rib and gully system of Bear Buttress. Forty-five minutes.

Ascent: Gain the first rib by traversing right from about 10m or so up the scree of the gully and follow it over gendarmes until below a maze of ribs and walls. Scramble directly up the rib above left, moving right onto heather to avoid its final step. Ascend the next rib, again turning the last section on the right, but this time more awkwardly.

Above is the blunt-fronted mass of Bear Tower. Scramble over ledges leading up to the right until below a group of overhangs (Crazy Pinnacle is at this level on the right). Now go precariously out left onto the nose to gain the top of the tower with a few breath-holding moves. The summit lies directly ahead above a mound of grass and stones.

Descent by this route: Not recommended.

Usual descents: Follow the clifftop path westwards, soon curving north, to a mine entrance. Turn right and descend north-east then east to join the approach at the stream which drains Cwm Du.

Accident Check List

Check Breathing
* If necessary clear airway using a hooked finger to remove obstructions - vomit, blood, teeth etc.
* Turn casualty to lie in the recovery position (unless you suspect spinal injury). This helps to maintain a clear airway.

Check for Severe Bleeding
* Apply direct pressure from a pad to stop bleeding.
* Elevate the limb.

Check for Broken Bones
* Do not move the casualty if a spinal injury is suspected.
* Immobilise other fractures using improvised splints and slings.

Monitor Condition
* Keep casualty warm and comfortable while awaiting rescue (protect from wind and insulate from ground).
* Reassure casualty and monitor condition regularly.

To Alert Mountain Rescue
Dial 999, ask for police/mountain rescue, and try to have the following written details ready:
* Precise position of the injured person on the crag.
* Location of the crag (including grid reference if possible).
* Time and nature of accident.

* Extent of injuries.
* Indication of prevailing weather at the scene (cloud base, wind strength, visibility etc.).
* Remain by the phone until met by a police officer or member of the rescue team.

Rescue Helicopters
* Secure all loose equipment before arrival of helicopter (weight rucksacks, jackets etc. with stones).
* Identify yourself by raising your arms in a V as helicopter approaches. Do **not** wave.
* Protect injured person from rotor downdraught (which is intense).
* Allow winchman to land of his own accord.
* Do not approach helicopter unless directed to do so by one of the crew (danger from rotors, exhaust etc.).

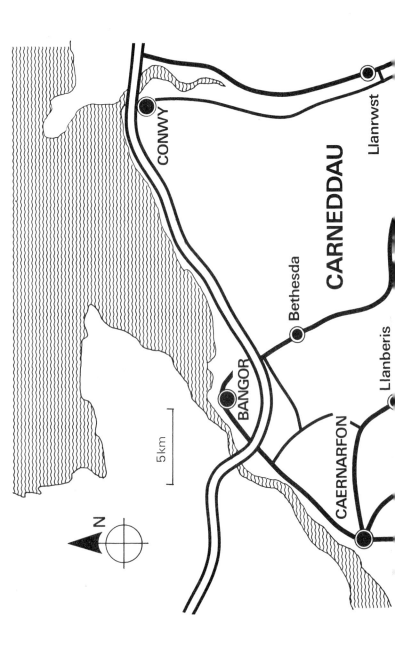